Welcoming
the Way
of the
Cross

Published by
The Bible Reading Fellowship
15 The Chambers, Vineyard
Abingdon OX14 3FE
United Kingdom
Tel: +44 (0)1865 319700
Email: enquiries@brf.org.uk
Website: www.brf.org.uk
BRF is a Registered Charity

ISBN 978 0 85746 180 3

First published 2013
10 9 8 7 6 5 4 3 2 1

Acknowledgments
Unless otherwise stated, scripture quotations are taken from the New Revised Standard
Version of the Bible, Anglicised edition, copyright © 1989, 1995 by the Division of Christian
Education of the National Council of the Churches of Christ in the United States of America,
and are used by permission. All rights reserved.

The extract from a poem by Eva Heymann is taken from *The Deeper Centre* © Darton, Longman
and Todd Ltd, 2006, and is used by kind permission of the publishers.

Cover photo: Tom Stoddart Archive/Getty Images

A catalogue record for this book is available from the British Library

Printed and bound by CPI Group (UK) Ltd, Croydon CR0 4YY

Welcoming
the Way
of the
Cross

Barbara Mosse

**A journey from Ash Wednesday
to Easter Day**

To Gerald,
friend and 'companion on the way',
with love and thanks.

Acknowledgments

*My thanks to Naomi Starkey for her support and enthusiasm
and editorial expertise; to my husband Martin for his patient
reading of the text, his constructive criticism and consistent
encouragement; and to the Revd Simon Sayers and the
congregations of the Anglican and Methodist churches in
Emsworth, Hampshire, who some years ago were the participants
in my 'Welcoming the Stranger' Lent course, which formed the
starting point for this book.*

Contents

Introduction

Nothing in my hand I bring,
Simply to thy Cross I cling;
Naked, come to thee for dress;
Helpless, look to thee for grace;
Foul, I to the fountain fly;
Wash me, Saviour, or I die.

A.M. TOPLADY (1740–78)

A challenging truth confronts us at the beginning of Lent, one graphically described above in the words of the well-known traditional hymn, 'Rock of ages'. While we may assent with our minds to Jesus' teaching that those who wish to be his disciples must deny themselves, take up their cross and follow him (Mark 8:34), something deep within us revolts against the demand for such a level of renunciation. When we encounter some of the implications of this teaching as expressed in the words of this hymn, part of us wants to recoil and dismiss such ideas as old-fashioned. Surely I have something to bring? A (mostly) good nature? Strength of character (maybe some of the time)? A willingness to be known as a Christian (as long as it doesn't 'rock the boat' too much)? And how healthy is it to think of myself as 'foul'? Surely I can't be as bad as all that?

When I was growing up, my church's teaching on the value of the lessons of Lent was patchy. Great emphasis was laid upon the virtue of 'giving something up', but it had to be something you really liked, or it didn't count. The season then became an exercise in how long, and how successfully (or not), I could hold out. Some years, I would arrive at Easter Day with a feeling of great pride and self-congratulation, and I would celebrate with an orgy of chocolate; other years left me feeling miserable at my failure—and I would console myself with an orgy of chocolate. Both end results missed the point: in neither case was I helped to appreciate a deeper link between giving up chocolate for Lent and Jesus' teaching about the cost of discipleship. After all, it was easy enough to give up chocolate for Lent if I could hold on to my pride and self-satisfaction by doing so (especially if my friend didn't manage it).

For those who want to save their life will lose it, and those who lose their life for my sake, and for the sake of the gospel, will save it. (Mark 8:35)

In 2005, the BBC broadcast a series involving a deeper kind of renunciation. It was called *The Monastery* and followed five men from very different backgrounds who were attempting to live for 40 days as postulant monks at Worth Abbey, a Roman Catholic Benedictine community in West Sussex. Not all had a religious background but all had applied to be part of the programme because they recognised in some way a lack of depth, direction and purpose in their lives. They all expressed this growing awareness differently but their shared hope was that their time in the monastery might help them in their quest for a way of life that had deeper meaning, purpose and integrity.

The first big step was in the willing renunciation (albeit temporarily) of their familiar lives and securities. They were asked to embrace a very different life pattern, one governed by the prayer, silence and work that formed the rhythm of the monastic day. Within that larger pattern were smaller renunciations: the submission to the discipline of the monastic routine, and the respect and use of prayerful silence, a concept foreign to most of the men. After they had had time to settle into life at the Abbey, the abbot requested that they relinquish their mobile phones—their lifeline to their usual lives—for the remainder of their time there. All but one agreed.

It was evident from the overwhelming public response to *The Monastery* that the inner journeys undertaken by the five men struck a near-universal chord. Increasingly rapid developments in communications and information technology have not resulted in the increased hours of leisure time that were confidently promised; rather, our lives have become ever busier and the demands of our workplaces insatiable. Money and possessions have not made us happier, only greedy for more and envious of those who seem to have more than we do. For many, the 'rat race' is more of a reality than ever as we juggle the relentless and incessant demands of work, family and leisure. The ever-increasing demands on GPs' surgeries underline the reality of stress as a chronic problem, and there are very few areas of our lives today untouched by it. Increasing numbers of people are now able to work from home, but, despite the speed of communications and the vast amount of information now available at the touch of a button, the space and time for refreshment and renewal still somehow elude us. Even the church is not immune. With a tendency to hype, over-activity and an anxious need to be seen as 'successful' and 'relevant', it often evades the challenge to model a view of life with radically different values that would enable deeper, more authentic ways of being in the world.

Yet there *is* another voice, to which *The Monastery* bears witness, making itself heard amid the clamour of society's inner and outer noise. It offers the glimpse of a way of life where, quite literally, 'less is more', a way of life that radically challenges our excessive consumerism and general over-activity. The need for space—healing, renewing, revitalising space in which the body can be rested and the spirit fed—is not so easily quenched by the noisy demands that at times threaten to overwhelm. The volunteers for *The Monastery* are not alone. On one level, the television series was a very public experiment—a sort of religious reality show. At a more profound level, though, it made visible a search that is universal, a search not confined simply to those who have a strongly developed religious consciousness. Monasteries, convents and retreat houses throughout the world bear witness to a huge upsurge of interest in what they have to offer. People of all ages, from all walks of life and of all faiths and none, are seeking out these places of rest and retreat. They are recognising, however inarticulately, the urgent need to pay attention to the deep well of inner longing, and to the fact that heeding the still, small voice within is, at the deepest level of being, the way to abundant life and wholeness.

We know, however, that it is not quite that straightforward. This longing for space and time apart is double-edged: we both yearn for it and fear it. We recognise that all our acquisitiveness does not satisfy us and that the emptiness within draws us and compels our attention; and yet at the same time we recoil, fearful of the challenges we may be called upon to face. We are accustomed to constant noise and distraction, and we fear that, if thrown back simply on our inner resources, we will find only emptiness there.

This Lent we have an opportunity to explore some of the

ways we may be encouraged to let go and learn to trust the still, small voice of God within. With the help of scripture, we will explore some of the situations that encourage us to 'take up our cross'—situations that prompt us to seek a different way of living and a deeper, more authentic relationship with God. Along the way we will also explore some of the spaces outside ourselves that somehow resonate with the 'God-space'[1] within, and their mysterious possibilities for growth and transformation. When we create a space for the other—whether that other be God, our fellow human beings or our own inner shadow side—we are, essentially, welcoming the way of the cross. We are responding to the challenge to live with an open heart, to set aside the priority of our own interests and concerns, recognising that when we welcome the other, we will inevitably be affected and changed by the relationship. It is a risky business: we cannot know at the outset how we will be changed, only that we are opening ourselves up to mystery.

This is possible for us only when we first know ourselves to be loved and accepted. In the early stages of *The Monastery*, Gary, one of the volunteers, was asked for his first thoughts and reactions. He said, most movingly, that in the welcome he had received at the Abbey he had encountered a depth of love and acceptance for him as a person, warts and all, that he had never before experienced. The love and acceptance of the monks was modelling for him something of the unconditional love of God, giving him the courage and hope to risk venturing more deeply on his own inner journey.

'We love, because he first loved us' (1 John 4:19). From Ash Wednesday to the first Sunday of Lent, we will therefore focus on the primary love of God for us and the place of welcome he continually offers within that love. This truth is pictured, beautifully and profoundly, in the life and ministry of Jesus, in the parable of the prodigal son (Luke 15:11–32). Week 1 begins with Jesus being 'driven' into the desert by the Holy Spirit and continues with an exploration of some of the different ways we may be asked to enter into that desert experience. Week 2 considers our lives of prayer as a response to God's first love for us, as we open our hearts to him in hope and trust. In Week 3 we consider 'spaces of welcome'—places that have the potential to reflect to us something of the loving self-giving and acceptance of God. We rejoice in the gift of creation in all its beauty and variety, and in the wonder of sacred spaces and places that have power to evoke our ancient longings.

An encounter with our shadow side is inevitable if we are serious about prayer as an offering of space and welcome to God, and in Week 4 we will spend some time reflecting on the kind of feelings that may emerge when we become aware of our poverty and weakness in comparison with his glory and majesty. In Week 5 we turn our attention outwards to the world. We will look at situations that invite us to take up our cross—in the solitary path of prayer and contemplation within the body of Christ, in the love and care of neighbour, and in the work of mission. The challenging days of Holy Week offer us an opportunity to walk closely with some who were present, inviting us to identify with their pain, suffering and confusion as they move through the darkness of the passion before emerging into the glorious light of Easter morning.

The pieces for Weeks 1 to 5 are accompanied by a scripture text as a basis for personal prayer, and a question for further reflection. Holy Week itself has been left free of questions, to allow for deeper personal reflection on the Bible passage for the day. At the end of the book, all the questions have been grouped together under their respective 'Weeks' for the purposes of group study.

'Nothing in my hand I bring, simply to thy Cross I cling.' We can bring nothing to God of our own, other than the poverty and neediness of our naked selves; and our journey, like Christ's, lies through the cross. This season of Lent invites us to welcome the way of the cross in whatever guise it may come, through joy and sadness, pain and delight, through the actions of friend and enemy. It challenges us to deepen our discipleship and open our eyes to seek God everywhere, under whatever disguise he may be concealed, and in so doing to gradually learn to renounce the false idols we repeatedly attempt to put in God's place. It is a journey not just for Lent but for a lifetime, a journey that invites us to marvel at the divine energy which cannot be contained but overflows into the creation in an eternal dynamic of exuberant life and costly, self-giving love.

Love (III)

Love bade me welcome: yet my soul drew back,
  Guilty of dust and sin.
But quick-ey'd Love, observing me grow slack
  From my first entrance in,
Drew nearer to me, sweetly questioning,
  If I lack'd anything.

A guest, I answer'd, worthy to be here:
  Love said, You shall be he.
I, the unkind, the ungrateful? Ah my dear,
  I cannot look on thee.
Love took my hand, and smiling did reply,
  Who made the eyes but I?

Truth, Lord, but I have marr'd them: let my shame
  Go where it doth deserve.
And know you not, says Love, who bore the blame?
  My dear, then I will serve.
You must sit down, says Love, and taste my meat:
  So I did sit and eat.

GEORGE HERBERT (1593–1633)

Ash Wednesday to Saturday

Because he first loved us

The long road home

Then Jesus said, 'There was a man who had two sons. The younger of them said to his father, "Father, give me the share of the property that will belong to me." So he divided his property between them. A few days later the younger son gathered all he had and travelled to a distant country, and there he squandered his property in dissolute living. When he had spent everything, a severe famine took place throughout that country, and he began to be in need. So he went and hired himself out to one of the citizens of that country, who sent him to his fields to feed the pigs. He would gladly have filled himself with the pods that the pigs were eating; and no one gave him anything. But when he came to himself he said, "How many of my father's hired hands have bread enough and to spare, but here I am dying of hunger! I will get up and go to my father, and I will say to him, 'Father, I have sinned against heaven and before you; I am no longer worthy to be called your son; treat me like one of your hired hands.'" So he set off and went to his father. But while he was still far off, his father saw him and was filled with compassion; he ran and put his arms around him and kissed him. Then the son said to him, "Father, I have sinned against heaven and before you; I am no longer worthy to be called your son." But the father said to his slaves, "Quickly, bring out a robe—the best one—and put it on him; put a ring on his finger and sandals on his feet. And get the fatted calf and kill it, and let us eat and celebrate; for this son of mine was dead and is alive again; he was lost and is found!" And they began to celebrate.'

LUKE 15:11–24

This familiar and well-loved parable from Luke's Gospel is known to us by many names—the 'prodigal son', the 'waiting/compassionate father' and the 'two sons', among others. This reflects the fact that the parable offers us a rich and multi-layered text, all the facets of which would take a lifetime to exhaust. The American theologian R. Alan Culpepper describes it in this way: 'It is no simple simile with a single point but a compressed slice of life with complexity and texture.'[2] Today we focus our gaze on one particular facet—the impetuous younger son and his relationship with his father. Later in the season (Week 4, Sunday), we will turn our attention to his elder brother.

We begin our Lenten journey at a moment of family crisis. In a few brief, unvarnished words, Luke introduces the three main characters of the story and, without further ado, plunges us into an atmosphere of tension and misunderstanding. We are not given any 'backstory' for these characters, so we do not know what has prompted the younger son to demand his share of the property so abruptly from his father. At the very least, the request was selfish, disrespectful and irregular; at worst, it was tantamount to wishing his father dead. But without any argument or attempt to reason with his son, the father does what he has been asked and the son 'gathered all he had and travelled to a distant country' (v. 13).

The pattern that follows is perhaps all too predictable—the riotous, immoral living; the artificial, wealth-induced popularity; the disappearance of the son's fair-weather friends once all his money has gone; the consequent descent into shame, degradation and near-despair. The decision to return to his father's house and seek the position of a servant is prompted not so much by remorse as by the realisation that he had, quite literally, nowhere else to go.

It is at this point, perhaps, that we need to make a special attempt to reflect on this story as if for the first time. It may well be that the younger son's experience holds no real surprises for us, but the reaction of his father on his return should stun us into deeper attention. Here we find no angry words, no reproaches or recriminations, no sense of 'I told you so'. On seeing his son 'while he was still far off', his father runs out to meet him and welcomes him back with compassion, love and forgiveness. The son's request that he be treated like one of the hired servants is completely ignored as the father gives urgent and immediate instructions for the celebration.

Rembrandt's hauntingly memorable painting captures the power and poignancy of their reconciliation. The son, his sandals and tunic shabby and tattered, kneels at his father's feet, his strength utterly spent. He leans his head on his father's breast as the father reaches forward, gathering his son into a welcoming embrace of total love and forgiveness.

Like the younger son, we need to come to a point where we realise that the long road home is the only option we have. But it is a journey we will not accomplish overnight: our inbuilt resistance to acknowledging our inner poverty and total dependence on God means that we have to relearn our need over and over again. As we open ourselves to the way of the cross, this parable challenges us to see ourselves in the place of the prodigal as we turn back to our loving heavenly Father, trusting that in his love and forgiveness he will never turn us away.

Henri Nouwen came to this realisation personally when he encountered Rembrandt's painting at a particularly low point in his life. He had just finished a demanding lecture trip and was totally exhausted. During the trip he had felt strong and in control, but afterwards was left feeling needy and vulnerable.

> *It was in this condition that I first encountered Rembrandt's* Prodigal Son... *After my long, self-exposing journey, the tender embrace of father and son expressed everything I desired at that moment... Now I desired only to rest safely in a place where I could feel a sense of belonging, a place where I could feel at home.*[3]

For reflection and prayer

There is no fear in love, but perfect love casts out fear; for fear is to do with punishment, and whoever fears has not reached perfection in love. We love because he first loved us.

1 JOHN 4:18–19

A question

'You are my beloved son/daughter.' At the beginning of our Lenten journey to the cross and beyond, are we able to take these words into our hearts as God's personal affirmation of love for us?

Thursday

Home is where we start from

Rebekah took the best garments of her elder son Esau, which were with her in the house, and put them on her younger son Jacob; and she put the skins of the kids on his hands and on the smooth part of his neck. Then she handed the savoury food, and the bread that she had prepared, to her son Jacob.

So he went in to his father, and said, 'My father'; and he said, 'Here I am; who are you, my son?' Jacob said to his father, 'I am Esau your firstborn. I have done as you told me; now sit up and eat of my game, so that you may bless me.' But Isaac said to his son, 'How is it that you have found it so quickly, my son?' He answered, 'Because the Lord your God granted me success.' Then Isaac said to Jacob, 'Come near, that I may feel you, my son, to know whether you are really my son Esau or not.' So Jacob went up to his father Isaac, who felt him and said, 'The voice is Jacob's voice, but the hands are the hands of Esau.' He did not recognise him, because his hands were hairy like his brother Esau's hands; so he blessed him.

GENESIS 27:15–23

The incident described in today's passage, where Jacob steals the blessing of his father Isaac from under the nose of his elder twin Esau, graphically presents us with one of the 'highlights' (if we may call it that) in the life of an archetypal dysfunctional family. The marriage of Isaac and Rebekah appears to have been one of genuine love, at least on Isaac's side (Genesis 24:67), but the couple's happiness had been blighted by the reality of Rebekah's barrenness. The twins were conceived after Jacob had prayed to the Lord for his wife, but the early signs were ominous. Rebekah had become aware of the two children struggling together within her womb (25:22) and, on asking the Lord about it, she was told, 'Two nations are in your womb, and two peoples born of you shall be divided; one shall be stronger than the other, the elder shall serve the younger' (v. 23). The two boys, once born, could not have been more different: Esau the elder, 'all his body like a hairy mantle' (v. 25), was a rough outdoor type and a skilful hunter, 'while Jacob was a quiet man, living in tents' (v. 27). Family tension was further compounded as its members split along the lines dictated by parental favouritism: 'Isaac loved Esau, because he was fond of game; but Rebekah loved Jacob' (v. 28).

Many years of tension and discord have led up to the event we read about today. But if we are tempted to think that Esau is the innocent victim here, we would do well to remember just how cheaply he held the value of his birthright as Jacob's eldest son, when he sold it to Jacob in exchange for a bowl of stew (vv. 29–34).

The unpredictable factors of our background can have a powerful influence on the course our lives eventually take. Some years ago, when I was working in prison chaplaincy, I met a prisoner who was known to everyone as Big Jim. Big he was, in every sense of the word—a giant of a man. For years, his reputation within the prison system had been terrible. The product of a wretched childhood, Jim had been sentenced to life for shooting a policeman in the 1960s. He had been moved many times round the prison system since then and had earned a reputation as a violent and ruthless man. Whenever there was a protest within the prison, you could guarantee that Big Jim would be behind it as the chief instigator and rabble-rouser.

At the time of our meeting, though, there had been a dramatic change. A couple of years previously, Jim had encountered Christ in the most profound way—a meeting that had turned his life around every bit as dramatically as had Paul's meeting with Christ on the road to Damascus. Big Jim had been feared by all, but he now became a person whom other people, both fellow prisoners and staff, would seek out for his loving wisdom and counsel. He would speak of his past actions with a sense of deep sorrow and regret; at the same time, his belief in the forgiving and healing love of Christ in his life was unshakeable. Hard-bitten prison officers who had known Jim for years as an angry, bitter, dangerous man found their natural cynicism and suspicion overwhelmed when he spoke of his experience with such honesty, transparency and conviction. The love of God shone out of him and there could hardly have been a more powerful witness to the power of Christ to heal and transform.

Whoever we are, 'home' is, indeed, where we start from; and it all seems completely random. We have no say in whether we are born male or female, into poverty or plenty, into what geographical area or during what period of history. Many of us will be fortunate enough to know the happiness and security of a loving home and the good and confident start it gives us in life; for others, this will be very far from the case. Either way, we can take great encouragement from the lives of people such as Jacob and Big Jim, because their difficult early experiences were clearly no barrier to the healing and redeeming work of God. As we ponder the complex mixture of weakness and strength, sinfulness and goodness that made up their lives, we see the reflection of our own fragile and vulnerable humanity. And as their flawed humanity was forgiven and transformed within the healing love of God, so too can ours.

For reflection and prayer

I waited patiently for the Lord; he inclined to me and heard my cry. He drew me up from the desolate pit, out of the miry bog, and set my feet upon a rock, making my steps secure. He put a new song in my mouth, a song of praise to my God. Many will see and fear, and put their trust in the Lord.

PSALM 40:1–3

A question

George Herbert's poem, 'Love (III)' (see page 13), gives us a particularly intense and intimate expression of what 'home' could mean. What kinds of feelings does the poem touch in you? How easy do we find it to allow God to love us in this way?

Friday

For it was you who formed me

O Lord, you have searched me and known me. You know when I sit down and when I rise up; you discern my thoughts from far away. You search out my path and my lying down, and are acquainted with all my ways...

Where can I go from your spirit? Or where can I flee from your presence? If I ascend to heaven, you are there; if I make my bed in Sheol, you are there. If I take the wings of the morning and settle at the farthest limits of the sea, even there your hand shall lead me, and your right hand shall hold me fast...

For it was you who formed my inward parts; you knit me together in my mother's womb. I praise you, for I am fearfully and wonderfully made... My frame was not hidden from you, when I was being made in secret, intricately woven in the depths of the earth. Your eyes beheld my unformed substance. In your book were written all the days that were formed for me, when none of them as yet existed...

O that you would kill the wicked, O God, and that the bloodthirsty would depart from me – those who speak of you maliciously, and lift themselves up against you for evil! ... Search me, O God, and know my heart; test me and know my thoughts.

PSALM 139:1–3, 7–10, 13–16, 19–20, 23 (ABRIDGED)

The heading to this psalm claims that it is 'of David', and in it the author affirms his faith and trust while surrounded by forces hostile both to himself (v. 19) and to God (vv. 20–22). Over-sensitive lectionary compilers sometimes omit verses 19–22 from public readings of this psalm, deeming the sentiments expressed to be somehow 'unChristian'. But if we do omit them, we diminish the impact of the psalm in several ways. First, we lose that which gives the psalm its essential context—a turning to God who is all-seeing, all-knowing and all-caring, by one who feels trapped in a situation bristling with danger and hostility, who is also aware of the frailty and waywardness of his own thoughts and attitudes (vv. 22–24). Second, such omissions collude with our own desire to suppress those primitive, uncontrollable emotions that can arise in situations where we believe ourselves to be 'under attack'.

We may find ourselves in sympathy with the author, both in his sense of being surrounded by hostile forces and in his plea to God, and yet still we may feel a little uneasy. Several decades ago, the actress and comedian Joyce Grenfell wrote and performed a song called 'The right to be private'. This was around the time when people were becoming aware of the potentialities of early computer development, and the new technology was beginning to find its way into the public arena. Like all of Joyce Grenfell's work, the song combined wit and humour but was also laced with a prophetic awareness of some of the then-unknown horizons to which the new technology would take us. Much of what Joyce Grenfell foresaw in that song has subsequently come to be, and we now live in a world where personal privacy is an increasingly rare and greatly prized commodity. Supermarket loyalty cards may well offer substantial savings on the increasingly expensive weekly shop, but at the same time they record our preferences and store our personal details in order to encourage us to spend even more. When we are out and about, CCTV cameras track our every move—a reality we may find reassuring when it has a positive effect in terms of crime prevention and reduction, but less so when such surveillance invades our own privacy.

'O Lord, you have searched me and known me… and are acquainted with all my ways' (vv. 1, 3). In our bad moments, these words may resonate with our nervousness about the invasion of privacy, suggesting the idea of God as some sort of celestial 'Big Brother'. This may cause us some uneasiness, at least on the unconscious level. As disciples of Christ we may honestly wish to grow in our relationship to God and desire an increasing closeness to him, yet we still shrink from the experience of naked exposure that such closeness inevitably brings with it. God 'searches us out', and there may well be parts of ourselves that we would rather he didn't search! However hard we work to convince ourselves otherwise, we suspect, deep down, that we carry much within ourselves that would not easily bear the light of his scrutiny. The theologian David Bland has commented that this psalm 'comforts the afflicted and afflicts the comfortable',[4] and, in our struggles along the path of Christian discipleship, we may experience both parts of that equation at different times. It is inevitable that in this life, to some extent, our attitude will always be touched by a degree of ambivalence.

Despite this ambivalence, however, the psalm continues to offer us a tremendous source of comfort. None of us goes through life without experiencing times of suffering, illness and bereavement, and it is at times like these that we may become particularly aware of a sense of aloneness, even when we are surrounded by loving support. These verses offer the assurance that even in such times of darkness, the loving presence of God is constant: 'If I say, "Surely the darkness will cover me, and the light around me become night", even the darkness is not dark to you; the night is as bright as the day, for darkness is as light to you' (vv. 11–12).

In his great exposition of Christian love, Paul expresses brilliantly the pain and ambiguity of our partial awareness: 'For now we see in a mirror, dimly, but then we will see face to face. Now I know only in part; then I will know fully, even as I have been fully known' (1 Corinthians 13:12).

For reflection and prayer

Thus says God, the Lord, who created the heavens and stretched them out... I am the Lord, I have called you in righteousness, I have taken you by the hand and kept you; I have given you as... a light to the nations, to open the eyes that are blind, to bring out... from the prison those who sit in darkness.

ISAIAH 42:5–7 (ABRIDGED)

A question

'O Lord, you have searched me and known me... and are acquainted with all my ways.' How do these words of the psalmist make you feel? Do you want God to be 'acquainted with all your ways'?

Saturday

'You are my beloved Son'

John the baptiser appeared in the wilderness, proclaiming a baptism of repentance for the forgiveness of sins... He proclaimed, 'The one who is more powerful than I is coming after me; I am not worthy to stoop down and untie the thong of his sandals. I have baptised you with water, but he will baptise you with the Holy Spirit.'

In those days Jesus came from Nazareth of Galilee and was baptised by John in the Jordan. And just as he was coming up out of the water, he saw the heavens torn apart and the Spirit descending like a dove on him. And a voice came from heaven, 'You are my Son, the Beloved; with you I am well pleased.'

MARK 1:4, 7–11 (ABRIDGED)

John baptises Jesus in the River Jordan and immediately we hit a stumbling-block: if the baptism that John was offering really was 'a baptism of repentance for the forgiveness of sins' (v. 4), then how do we understand the action of Jesus—the sinless one—in coming to John for baptism? Matthew's fuller account emphasises the paradox. There, John tries to deter Jesus from baptism, and his response to Jesus shows that he is clearly confused by his request: 'I need to be baptised by you, and do you come to me?' (Matthew 3:14). Jesus' response, 'Let it be so now; for it is proper for us in this way to fulfil all righteousness' (v. 15), can hardly be said to throw instant light on the matter. Throughout history, theologians and commentators have struggled to understand what was really going on here. Was Jesus subject to sin up to this point? Or was he simply making a public identification of himself with the rest of sinful humanity? Such critical exploration is vitally important but we are not going to attempt here to add to the fruit of these studies. Rather, we are going take Jesus' advice and 'let it be so now', focusing instead on one specific statement: 'You are my Son, the Beloved; with you I am well pleased' (Mark 1:11b).

The voice from heaven is common to Matthew, Mark and Luke, with one small but very significant difference. Whereas Matthew 3:17 has the voice addressing the witnesses ('This is my Son, the Beloved'), in Mark and in Luke 3:22, the address is made directly to Jesus ('You are my Son, the Beloved'). Why did this need saying—and why might Jesus have needed to hear it? The personal form of the statement is consistent with the idea that Jesus grew only gradually into his sense of vocation, with significant points along the way that slowly enabled him to discern the unique shape his calling was to take. An earlier such incident would seem to be the visit to Jerusalem when Jesus was twelve years old: there was no heavenly voice on that occasion, simply a precociously mature realisation that his priority was to be about his Father's business (Luke 2:49).

In each of the first three Gospels, Jesus' baptism immediately precedes his time of testing in the wilderness, and it is hard to escape the conclusion that at this crucial point in his life, Jesus needed the absolute reassurance that he was, indeed, God's beloved Son. The path on which he was set was to be one of obedient suffering, one where his willing acceptance of the escalating loneliness and rejection that came with his vocation would climax in his passion and death on the cross.

If Jesus needed the reassurance of his Father's love—a reassurance that enabled him to welcome the way that would lead to the cross—how much more is that true of us. We know in our minds that 'we love because he first loved us', but embracing that glorious truth in the innermost depths of our hearts is often another thing entirely.

In his beautiful and powerful poem, 'Love (III)', George Herbert captures our difficulty precisely. God welcomes the poet—the sinner—and invites him to sit down and eat. The sinner protests because he knows himself to be 'guilty of dust and sin' and therefore estranged from God, completely unworthy of his love. God acknowledges the sinner's problem but points him directly to Christ, saying, 'Know you not who bore the blame?' The impulse of God to forgiveness and open-hearted, loving acceptance is overwhelming and irresistible. As the sinner is gently coaxed into the embrace of God's love, he discovers a depth of forgiveness, understanding and acceptance that he would never have thought possible.

Yet there is more for us to ponder and wonder at in George Herbert's graphic word-picture. The loving invitation extended to the sinner is no grudging welcome but one that is generous and forgiving, holding nothing back. We are reminded irresistibly of the father's welcome of the returning prodigal. The sinner's initial reaction also rings true to us: we are sinners, so how can we possibly be worthy of such love? Perhaps the moment when we realise that we can never deserve God's love or earn it in any way is the moment when our 'journey home' truly begins.

'Do not fear, for I have redeemed you; I have called you by name, you are mine... you are precious in my sight, and honoured, and I love you' (Isaiah 43:1, 4). With these words we have come full circle and find ourselves back with Herbert's poem—and with the Father's calling of his Son at his baptism. God calls each one of us, as he called Christ, to welcome the way of the cross, whatever the shape or pattern it takes in our lives. We are invited to follow that way in trust and confidence, secure in the assurance that our Father loves us with an everlasting love and that, whatever happens, he will never let us go.

For reflection and prayer
I have loved you with an everlasting love.
JEREMIAH 31:3

A question
In another Gospel account, John the Baptist is reported as saying of Jesus, 'He must increase, but I must decrease' (John 3:30). How easy do you find it to hand over areas of your work for others to take on?

Week 1

Into the desert

Sunday

'If you are the Son of God...'

Then Jesus was led up by the Spirit into the wilderness to be tempted by the devil. He fasted for forty days and nights, and afterwards he was famished. The tempter came and said to him, 'If you are the Son of God, command these stones to become loaves of bread.' But he answered, 'It is written, "One does not live by bread alone, but by every word that comes from the mouth of God."'

Then the devil took him to the holy city and placed him on the pinnacle of the temple, saying to him, 'If you are the Son of God, throw yourself down; for it is written, "He will command his angels concerning you", and "On their hands they will bear you up, so that you will not dash your foot against a stone."' Jesus said to him, 'Again it is written, "Do not put the Lord your God to the test."'

Again, the devil took him to a very high mountain and showed him all the kingdoms of the world and their splendour; and he said to him, 'All these I will give you, if you will fall down and worship me.' Jesus said to him, 'Away with you, Satan! For it is written, "Worship the Lord your God, and serve only him."' Then the devil left him, and suddenly angels came and waited on him.

MATTHEW 4:1–11

How often does it happen in our own journey through life that the high points are immediately followed by a plunge into the depths? When someone is enjoying a spell of good fortune, faintly cynical comments such as 'Make the most of it, because it won't last', although unhelpful, would seem to echo something of this experience. We may think we would like to live our lives on a continuous high, but we know in our hearts that this could never be true to the reality of the way life actually is.

That reality is clearly patterned for us today in this episode in the life of Jesus. We have just witnessed the high point of his baptism, with all its reassurance and affirmation ('You are my Son, the Beloved; with you I am well pleased': Mark 1:11); and as Jesus now stands on the threshold of his public ministry, the Spirit leads him into the desert for a period of prolonged and sustained temptation. Both Luke and Matthew imply a non-traumatic onset to this time of testing, stating that the Spirit simply 'led' Jesus into the wilderness (Luke 4:1; Matthew 4:1). Mark's account is terse and concise: it does not detail the temptations and is described in only two verses (1:12–13). Despite this brevity, however, Mark, through the use of two particular words, manages to capture an intensity and sense of drama that the other two accounts miss. In Mark, the Spirit 'immediately drove' Jesus out into the wilderness. Jesus has just been baptised; divine reassurance and encouragement have been given, but he is allowed no time to relax and bask in the glow of it all. Impelled, *driven*, by the Spirit, Jesus immediately finds himself facing a time of grave temptation—and it would seem that the very movement into the desert itself was a struggle.

There is a strong element of compulsion in Mark's choice of words: people tend not to need 'driving' if the place and direction they are going is of their own choosing. The transition from the spiritual heights of the baptism to the trauma of the temptations is abrupt and discomfiting, but it is a transition that we would perhaps do well to ponder. The same sequence is followed in Matthew, Mark and Luke, suggesting an element of divine 'givenness' about this apparent cause-and-effect. Jesus calls people to follow him; it may be that the pattern of reassurance—temptation—reassurance that we see in Jesus' experience here indicates a more general pattern, relevant to all who choose to be his disciples.

The voice from heaven at Jesus' baptism affirms him as the beloved Son of God, and immediately the words of the devil (however we envisage him) plant a seed of doubt. The devil's words, 'If you are the Son of God...' precede the first two temptations, placing Jesus in a chilling, seemingly inescapable double-bind. 'If you are the Son of God... then prove it! Satisfy your hunger! Dazzle the multitudes with your miraculous abilities! Rule the world under my authority and protection!' It has sometimes been said that there was never any real doubt as to the outcome of Jesus' testing, but if that were the case, we would be reading about an illusion of temptation only. No—the three traditional temptations were real; we should make no mistake about that. Jesus was undoubtedly being offered the opportunity to take short-cuts and misuse his divine power, but the primary temptation that preceded these three struck at the very heart of his relationship with his Father: 'If you are the Son of God...' Only if Jesus doubted the fundamental reality of this Father–Son relationship would his yielding to the other temptations become possible.

This pattern of temptation may be one we recognise from our own experience of discipleship. We receive a powerful reassurance of God's love for us, and then the clouds descend and we do not feel so secure in that love. We are then perhaps tempted to look for props and short-cuts to bolster us up in our insecurity, rather than relying on the promises of God alone. By his insistent response, 'It is written...', Jesus models for each one of us the affirmation of what we know to be true, even when our feelings about that truth are under attack.

For reflection and prayer

'Simon, Simon, listen! Satan has demanded to sift all of you like wheat, but I have prayed for you that your own faith may not fail; and you, when once you have turned back, strengthen your brothers.'

LUKE 22:31

A question

Spend a little time reviewing the pattern of your life and the subtle shapes and forms that temptation takes within it. How do you recognise temptation when it occurs, and how do you attempt to deal with it?

Monday

A voice crying in
the wilderness

The beginning of the good news of Jesus Christ, the Son of God. As it is written in the prophet Isaiah, 'See, I am sending my messenger ahead of you, who will prepare your way; the voice of one crying out in the wilderness: "Prepare the way of the Lord, make his paths straight."' John the baptiser appeared in the wilderness, proclaiming a baptism of repentance for the forgiveness of sins. And people from the whole Judean countryside and all the people of Jerusalem were going out to him, and were baptised by him in the river Jordan, confessing their sins. Now John was clothed with camel's hair, with a leather belt around his waist, and he ate locusts and wild honey.

MARK 1:1–6

Over the last two days, we have spent some time considering Jesus' time of temptation in the wilderness and the event that preceded it in the Gospel accounts—his baptism in the river Jordan by John. Today we take a further step back and reflect on John himself and his desert environment as he erupted on to the Gospel stage.

The early life of John the Baptist is shrouded in mystery. Mark's Gospel tells us nothing of what went before: it begins abruptly with today's passage and John's startling arrival in the public arena. In Matthew and John also, the Baptist arrives as a full-grown man with an urgent message for the people. Luke tells us a little more: chapter 1 records the 'annunciation' to his father Zechariah (vv. 5–23), the reaction of the baby in the womb when Mary visits his mother Elizabeth (vv. 39–45), the naming of the baby and Zechariah's prophecy regarding his vocation (vv. 59–79). Thereafter, states Luke, 'The child grew and became strong in spirit, and he was in the wilderness until the day he appeared publicly to Israel' (v. 80).

We do not know how John was in the wilderness from his early childhood, how he was cared for and taught, but we can be sure that the vocation to be 'a voice crying in the wilderness' was not an easy one. John's calling was essentially a calling to be a solitary—to be set apart from normal human society and generally misunderstood by it. In her book *Paths in Solitude*, the Christian solitary Eve Baker describes the work of the solitary/desert dweller as the task of attempting to hold together two worlds—the world that is the solitary's place of exile and the ordinary, workaday world from which he or she is exiled. Baker continues, 'Reconciliation of the two may be the task; always attempted but never achieved. The solitary is the voice crying in the wilderness; the cry is one of necessity, the burden which is imposed, whether or not the cry is heard.'[5]

The biblical understanding of 'desert' or 'wilderness' is far broader than the endless sand and scorching sun of popular imagination. The commonest Hebrew word for it, *midbar*, is used to refer to grassy pastures that support sheep (Psalm 65:12) and grass that gets burnt up by drought (Joel 1:19–20), but it is also used to describe desolate wastes of rock and sand (Deuteronomy 32:13). We find the same kind of variety in the use of the Greek term *eremos* in the New Testament

(Mark 1:3; see also Matthew 4:1; Luke 5:16; John 6:31). Mountains can also assume great significance in the desert landscape as places of God's revelation (see Exodus 3:1–6; 1 Kings 19:1–18; Matthew 15:29–38; 17:1–8).

Even before the desert experiences of Jesus and John the Baptist, the role of the desert as an intense testing-ground for character and vocation had ancient biblical roots. A large part of the Old Testament is given over to momentous desert experiences and their aftermath—the exodus from Egypt, followed by the Israelites 40 years' desert wandering on their way to the promised land and, later, the loss of that land through exile, leading to a complete re-evaluation of what they knew about God and their relationship with him. These were times of longing and rebellion, hope and despondency, a nostalgic yearning for an imagined golden past and a reaching out for the joyful promise of the future. They were often times of taking one step forward and two steps back; but, through the crucible of the desert experience, God loved and led his people, coaxing, rebuking and enabling them to learn (often through bitter experience) just how deeply they were loved.

So the desert, or the wilderness, offers a powerful image for our experiences of suffering, challenge and the divine call. Those who have visited a physical desert have experienced something of its particular power—the loneliness, the barren landscape, the lack of any of the comforts and stimulation with which we usually bolster and distract ourselves. With the lack of those usual securities, other voices may have a chance to begin to make themselves heard—the voices of the tempter, of our own inner compulsions, and of God.

As well as being a literal place, the desert can be understood as a significant aspect of our internal world. Quite apart from the involuntary desert experiences that overtake us in the normal course of life, such as bereavement, illness or divorce, the bracing challenge of the desert is available to anybody who chooses to create a regular time and space apart from the hurly-burly of life, to be alone with God. The wilderness may be a conscious part of our Lenten journey but it is inescapably a part of our wider Christian vocation. There are times when we are led (or driven) to enter the 'desert space' within, to lay aside our usual tendency to rely on our own resources and to look and listen, in hope and trust, to God alone.

For reflection and prayer

For God alone my soul waits in silence, for my hope is from him. He alone is my rock and my salvation, my fortress; I shall not be shaken.

PSALM 62:5–6

A question

How do you hold together the demands of the 'desert' and the demands of the 'marketplace' within your own life? Are there any ways in which the balance could be improved?

Tuesday

A thorn in the flesh

It is necessary to boast; nothing is to be gained by it, but I will go on to visions and revelations of the Lord. I know a person in Christ who fourteen years ago was caught up to the third heaven—whether in the body or out of the body I do not know; God knows. And I know that such a person—whether in the body or out of the body I do not know; God knows— was caught up into Paradise and heard things that are not to be told, that no mortal is permitted to repeat. On behalf of such a one I will boast, but on my own behalf I will not boast, except of my weaknesses. But if I wish to boast, I will not be a fool, for I will be speaking the truth. But I refrain from it, so that no one may think better of me than what is seen in me or heard from me, even considering the exceptional character of the revelations. Therefore, to keep me from being too elated, a thorn was given to me in the flesh, a messenger from Satan to torment me, to keep me from being too elated. Three times I appealed to the Lord about this, that it would leave me, but he said to me, 'My grace is sufficient for you, for power is made perfect in weakness.' So, I will boast all the more gladly of my weaknesses, so that the power of Christ may dwell in me.

2 CORINTHIANS 12:1–9

A number of years ago, I spent some time working as a Community Mental Health chaplain. The work was varied, challenging and rewarding, and I worked with local parish clergy, psychiatrists and community mental health teams across a wide geographical area. I also worked with many individuals in hospitals, clinics and their homes, one of whom was a man I shall name Trevor. A deeply committed Christian, Trevor was a highly intelligent, highly articulate man with a first-class Oxbridge degree. He had suffered from what in those days was called manic depression (MD) since his first year at university and was in his early 40s when I met him. The early days of his illness had been dark indeed: he had made two suicide attempts and credited his survival at that time to the intervention of an excellent psychiatrist who, along with providing medical treatment, managed to instil in him a sense of hope.

The pattern of Trevor's years since university had been chequered, and times of stability and the holding down of a good job alternated with periods when jobs were lost as the illness raged out of control. Through all of this, Trevor was determined to put his experience at the service of other people. He wrote booklets and papers for fellow MD sufferers and their carers, which were gratefully taken up and used by his own doctors. He gladly accepted invitations to talk to groups, where he was able to offer authentic hope and encouragement from within the reality of his own personal experience.

In today's reading, Paul moves from an attempt to describe the indescribable (his heavenly visions) to an all-too-earthly experience—his 'thorn in the flesh'. He clearly sees no need to elaborate, either because he felt it was not important to be specific or because his readers already knew what he meant and didn't need him to spell it out. Neither is it necessary for us to know whether this 'thorn' was a physical, emotional or psychological complaint; of far greater significance is its function and the role and purpose it signified in Paul's life. Whatever it was, Paul initially experienced it as a tormenting encumbrance, so much so that he made three unsuccessful requests that the Lord would remove it (v. 8). The reference to the thorn as 'a messenger of Satan' (v. 7) has troubled some commentators. It is possible that Paul had in mind the scenario we find in the book of Job, where Satan is given permission by God to probe and test Job's faith and resolution (Job 1:6–12). But whatever the origin of Paul's 'thorn', God was the one whom he believed to be in ultimate control, with the power to remove it or not, as he might choose. As time passed, Paul began to discern that the thorn itself, painful and difficult though it was, nevertheless formed a vital part of God's mysterious purposes in his life: '[The Lord] said to me, "My grace is sufficient for you, for power is made perfect in weakness." So, I will boast all the more gladly of my weaknesses, so that the power of Christ may dwell in me… for whenever I am weak, then I am strong' (vv. 9–10).

During our many discussions, I once asked Trevor if he ever wondered why the MD had developed, and whether he had ever prayed to be free of it. His thoughtful reply was striking:

There was a time when I prayed to be free of it, yes—and people at the church I attended at that time were certainly praying for me in that way. Well, for God's own good reasons, that kind of release didn't happen; but as time passed, I began to think about the MD very differently. This is going to sound very odd—but it began to feel as if I had been given some kind of dark and mysterious gift. Not a gift that I would wish on my worst enemy, but a gift, nonetheless. And I was being given a precious opportunity to plumb the deep riches and possibilities of that gift. So now I pray about it very differently, because the MD has become part of the fabric of my being, and it is one of the channels that God uses to enable me to share his love with others.

For reflection and prayer

We know that all things work together for good for those who love God, who are called according to his purpose.

ROMANS 8:28

A question

Is there anything in your life that you would identify as a 'thorn in the flesh'? What are you feelings about it, and how do you incorporate those feelings honestly into your prayer?

Wednesday

Inner poverty

When Jesus saw the crowds, he went up the mountain; and after he sat down, his disciples came to him. Then he began to speak, and taught them, saying,

'Blessed are the poor in spirit, for theirs is the kingdom of heaven.

'Blessed are those who mourn, for they will be comforted.

'Blessed are the meek, for they will inherit the earth.

'Blessed are those who hunger and thirst for righteousness, for they will be filled.

'Blessed are the merciful, for they will receive mercy.

'Blessed are the pure in heart, for they will see God.

'Blessed are the peacemakers, for they will be called children of God...

'Blessed are you when people revile you and persecute you and utter all kinds of evil against you falsely on my account. Rejoice and be glad, for your reward is great in heaven, for in the same way they persecuted the prophets who were before you.'

MATTHEW 5:1–10, 12

It has become customary in some circles (including some Christian circles) to view the part of Jesus' teaching known to us as the Beatitudes as wonderful poetry containing beautiful and admirable sentiments, but as being far too idealistic to offer a realistic pattern for living in our present age. After all, goes the familiar argument, if we really were that meek and 'poor in spirit', refusing to stand up for ourselves, what would happen? We would become doormats, and everybody else would trample all over us.

Yet those of us who truly seek to be disciples of Christ should not be satisfied to justify ourselves in this way or let ourselves off the hook so lightly. If we look a little closer at these words, we will see, possibly to our discomfort, that Jesus is not suggesting some pie-in-the-sky future state that is impossible to attain, but is addressing a situation current among his followers at that moment. Jesus says, 'Blessed *are* the poor in spirit... those who mourn... the meek...', not 'Blessed *will be...*'. The present tense is clearly intended to indicate something that is already true about the Christian community, at least potentially, and the subsequent use of the future tense ('for they will...') simply unfolds the natural consequences of what is already true.

But how is a state of such superhuman goodness possible for us? Surely sin will always get in the way, sabotaging even the very best of our intentions? In her book *Before the Living God*, the spirituality writer and Carmelite nun Ruth Burrows offers some thoughts and ideas that we don't often hear voiced from the pulpit. In words that could easily offer a meditation on the Beatitudes, she claims that God's principal work in us is to awaken in us true humility and poverty of spirit, and 'to make us deeply aware of our nothingness so that he can give himself to us. Everything depends on our willingness to stand in the truth, to refuse to escape from this painful revelation of self, to accept to stand naked before the living God.'[6]

The key here lies in 'our willingness to stand in the truth' of our weak and sinful self, and to face unflinchingly the unpalatable reality we see there. Most of us, most of the time, will go to great lengths to avoid this. We make excuses for ourselves; we overestimate (or underestimate) our capacities; anything rather than face up to our weakness and human frailty. Under this scrutiny, even our best motives can be revealed as fragile. Ruth Burrows continues, 'More and more I am given to see how self-love masquerades under love of the neighbour; how what appears to be the pure love and service of others is riddled with selfish motives.'[7] She describes how, earlier in her life, the realisation that her motives even for doing good were 'impure' distressed her greatly, but that she came to accept that this will always be an inevitable consequence of being human. 'Now I no longer expect or claim that anything I do is purely for God. I want it to be so and try for purity of heart but am content to see the smears of self.'[8]

Burrows is 'content to see the smears of self' because she has realised that only God can deal with the deep-rootedness of human sin and selfishness. I remember once getting quite anxious and distressed while praying, because of my persistent inability to deal with mental distractions. Surely I ought to be able to control my thoughts? A very wise spiritual director helped me to turn a corner when he said, 'Barbara, stop fretting! *Your* job is to turn up.' He was showing me that the real work of prayer belongs to God, and that it goes on deep in the soul of the one who is praying, far below the level of the inevitable surface worries and distractions. Similarly, inner peace came for Ruth Burrows when she was finally able to stop struggling and accept that the deepest work of purification in her belonged to God alone.

So our 'job', in our walk with God, is to 'turn up' and willingly enter the desert experience that precedes a calm and realistic acceptance of our human weakness. Ruth Burrows takes us right back to the spirit of the Beatitudes when she writes, 'In true love for our neighbour lies all the asceticism we need. Here is the way we die to self... Perfect love of the neighbour means complete death to self and the triumph of the life of Jesus in us.'[9] If we are truly seeking to grow in holiness, the means and the potential to do so lie very close at hand; we need look no further than the stuff of our ordinary daily lives. While we are in this life, even the best of our motives will always be mixed, but we can be at peace that it is so, and we can welcome with humility and gladness the gradual purification that God seeks to bring about in our hearts and lives.

For reflection and prayer

For thus said the Lord God, the Holy One of Israel: in returning and rest you shall be saved; in quietness and in trust shall be your strength.

ISAIAH 30:15

A question

Is it possible to live with genuine inner poverty while being materially comfortable? If so, how?

Thursday

A bridge between east and west

Do not fear, for I am with you; I will bring your offspring from the east, and from the west I will gather you; I will say to the north, 'Give them up,' and to the south, 'Do not withhold; bring my sons from far away and my daughters from the end of the earth—everyone who is called by my name, whom I created for my glory, whom I formed and made.'

ISAIAH 43:5–7

> *I cannot tell how he will win the nations,*
> *how he will claim his earthly heritage,*
> *how satisfy the needs and aspirations*
> *of east and west, of sinner and of sage.*
>
> 'I CANNOT TELL' (W.Y. FULLERTON, 1857–1932)

These words from a 20th-century hymn aptly and succinctly sum up one of the key problems of our age and of every age. In our supposedly sophisticated and mature world, where 'progress' tends to be the accepted watchword, nation still rises up against nation and we seem to be no nearer the reality of a true and lasting peace between nations and world faiths than we ever were. The church itself seems to fare no better. In these days, we endeavour to live out our Christian discipleship within a worldwide institution that not only struggles in its dialogue with other major world religions but also finds itself dealing with discord and misunderstanding between Christian East and Christian West, Catholic and Protestant, male and female, conservative and liberal within its own boundaries. In such a context (and every generation seems to have had its own forms of discord) the long-ago prophetic words of Baruch, foretelling the reunion of the scattered people of God, strike a note of particular poignancy.

Around the year 360, in the Roman province of Scythia Minor, a man was born who was destined to act as a significant bridge between the Christian religious experiences of East and West. John Cassian was the child of a wealthy and devout family. As a young man, he and an older friend, Germanus, entered a monastery in Bethlehem, close to the Cave of the Nativity. They were deeply impressed on hearing of the experience of one particular visitor to the monastery— Pinufius, a monk who had been living an austere and rigorous spiritual life in the Egyptian desert. So inspired were they by their visitor that Cassian and Germanus asked their superiors' permission to travel to Egypt, so that they might witness this way of life for themselves. They then spent seven years in the Egyptian desert, sitting at the feet of the monks who lived there and learning about their way of life.

Over the years, Christianity had gradually changed from a persecuted sect within Judaism to the accepted state religion, and many Christians had begun to feel that the faith had somehow lost its way as a result. Life had become too comfortable, too complacent, and a lot of the early vibrancy and challenge had dissipated. Men and women began to move out to the desert in increasing numbers to seek a life of poverty, simplicity and reliance on God alone. Deeply impressed by what he witnessed, Cassian returned from the desert and settled in Marseilles. There he wrote his two most famous works, the *Institutes* and the *Conferences*, based on his Egyptian experiences.

Cassian's intention was to bring the wisdom of the desert tradition into the West, in order to help deepen and revitalise its religious life, initially through the monasteries. So it is really from Cassian, who lived and worked so many centuries ago, that our present knowledge and experience of the desert tradition comes. Bearing fruit initially within the monastic system, the treasures of this tradition have blossomed and spread out down the centuries, and today they enrich many people from all walks of life on their own spiritual journeys.

Cassian's special gift was to teach a way of prayer nourished by the scriptures—in particular, the Psalms—and to see the monk's (or any Christian's) lifelong task as the establishment of the Christ-life within the heart. Cassian described the means of moving along this path as one of continuous prayer, in which prayer ceases to be an activity as such and, instead, gradually becomes the spiritual air in which the Christian lives and moves and breathes. This inspires and makes possible a life of discipleship that is inbreathed by the gospel, and the believer is united with Christ crucified in anticipation of the coming of the kingdom of God. Many theologians and mystics through the centuries have expressed aspects of this teaching in their own way and from within their own time, culture and environment, but it was Cassian who first became a bridge from the East, making desert spirituality available to enrich the spiritual traditions of the West.

In 1054, several centuries before the Reformation in Europe brought about the great Protestant–Catholic split, the Christian church in the East had split from that in the West amid a host of political, theological and ecclesiological differences. Although many institutional disagreements still stand between us, the life of continuous prayer, arising from the early desert tradition and disseminated initially through the teaching of Cassian, has for several centuries been healing the wounds of schism at the deeper level of prayer and the work of the Holy Spirit. At that level, we can confidently return to the words of the hymn with which we began, and follow the verse through to its conclusion in a genuine spirit of faith, hope and trust:

> *But this I know, all flesh shall see his glory,*
> *and he shall reap the harvest he has sown,*
> *and some glad day his sun will shine in splendour*
> *when the Saviour, Saviour of the world is known.*

For reflection and prayer

'All mine are yours, and yours are mine; and I have been glorified in them. And now I am no longer in the world, but they are in the world, and I am coming to you. Holy Father, protect them in your name that you have given me, so that they may be one, as we are one.'

JOHN 17:10–11

A question

In order to work towards the healing of divisions in our world, we need also to be open to the same work of healing within ourselves. How may we prepare ourselves for such a work of healing?

Friday

The burning bush

Moses was keeping the flock of his father-in-law Jethro, the priest of Midian; he led his flock beyond the wilderness, and came to Horeb, the mountain of God. There the angel of the Lord appeared to him in a flame of fire out of a bush; he looked, and the bush was blazing, yet it was not consumed. Then Moses said, 'I must turn aside and look at this great sight, and see why the bush is not burned up.' When the Lord saw that he had turned aside to see, God called to him out of the bush, 'Moses, Moses!' And he said, 'Here I am.' Then he said, 'Come no closer! Remove the sandals from your feet, for the place on which you are standing is holy ground.' He said further, 'I am the God of your father, the God of Abraham, the God of Isaac, and the God of Jacob.' And Moses hid his face, for he was afraid to look at God.

EXODUS 3:1–6

Today we enter the desert with Moses and consider it as a place of theophany—a place where God mysteriously makes himself known. For Moses, this theophany seems to occur when he least expects it: it happens in the midst of his ordinary daily routine, as he leads the flocks belonging to his father-in-law Jethro through the wilderness to fresh pasture at the foot of Mount Horeb. Horeb (known as Sinai elsewhere) is no ordinary mountain but is described as 'the mountain of God' (v. 1). Moses might be carrying out his usual routine but the location of this miracle heightens our expectation, prompting us to look for something of deeper than usual significance.

It would be a mistake to seek to understand the incident of the revelation of God in the burning bush through our normal categories of thinking. We are confronted with an angel, which anticipates the voice of God and prepares Moses to hear that voice, and a bush that burns but is not consumed by the flames. There are two parts to the revelation: first, the angel appears within the burning bush but does not speak; and second, once Moses' attention has been caught, the voice of God identifies himself as the God of Moses' ancestors and reminds Moses that the ground he stands on is holy.

The rest of chapters 3 and 4 give details of the very specific task that God allocated Moses (which Moses tries very hard to avoid!)—that of leading the Israelites out of their captivity in Egypt. We are not going to consider that discussion in detail here but will focus rather on the role that the desert experience plays in the prophet's formation. It is a familiar pattern, elements of which we have already seen earlier in the week, with Jesus' 40 days in the wilderness (Sunday) and the appearance of John the Baptist (Monday), and it is a pattern that transcends the centuries. Consider these words of Winston Churchill, taken from a book published in 1932:

Every prophet has to come from civilisation, but every prophet has to go into the wilderness. He must have a strong impression of a complex society and all that it has to give, and then he must serve periods of isolation and meditation. This is the process by which psychic dynamite is made.[10]

The fact that Churchill was writing out of his own experience of political isolation during the interwar years does not diminish the relevance of his words for our consideration of the desert experience today. As in the biblical material, there is a recognition of the interplay and relationship between the desert and the world, with the 'prophet' needing to have a foot in both camps. If the prophet can manage this sometimes difficult balance, then the voice of God (or Churchill's 'psychic dynamite') is able to break through.

The American Trappist monk Thomas Merton wrestled with his dual calling of hermit and writer for many years. Writing just over 20 years after Churchill, in 1953, Merton sees the need for a similar movement of human traffic between the desert and the world, and he highlights two particularly important points. First, our experience of the desert need not be a physical one; and second, a desert experience, of whatever type, is not something we can manufacture for ourselves but is God-ordained.

> I am speaking... of those who having led active and articulate lives in the world of men, leave their old life behind and go into the desert. The desert does not necessarily have to be physical—it can be found in the midst of men. But it is not found by human aspirations or idealism. It is mysteriously designated by the finger of God.[11]

Our attitude to the desert, whether it is literal or metaphorical, will always be characterised by a degree of ambivalence. The desert both attracts and repels. On the one hand it captures our imagination, drawing us onwards and ever deeper in our walk with God; yet on the other hand we fear it, knowing that in the desert we will become more aware of our weaknesses and failings and the shallowness and pettiness that so easily permeate our attitude and behaviour. We discover that the insincerity and pretence that characterise the masks we hide behind will be relentlessly stripped away, exposing us to the loving but critical scrutiny of the divine gaze. We find that 'it is a fearful thing to fall into the hands of the living God' (Hebrews 10:31) because in those hands there is, quite literally, nowhere to hide.

We may, like Moses, feel that we lack the strength and ability to own the truth of ourselves before God, but, if we can accept our naked vulnerability and helplessness before him, we will find that we are given the courage to respond. Then we too will be enabled to see 'the glory of the Lord' (Isaiah 60:1) and to continue on our way, inspired with renewed courage, fresh vision and rekindled hope.

For reflection and prayer

Then the Lord said to [Moses], 'Who gives speech to mortals? Who makes them mute or deaf, seeing or blind? Is it not I, the Lord? Now go, and I will be with your mouth and teach you what you are to speak.'

EXODUS 4:11–12

A question

Moses encountered God in the burning bush during the course of his normal daily work as a shepherd. Do we expect to encounter God amid the ordinariness of our daily routine?

In the beginning

In the beginning was the Word, and the Word was with God, and the Word was God. He was in the beginning with God. All things came into being through him, and without him not one thing came into being. What has come into being in him was life, and the life was the light of all people. The light shines in the darkness, and the darkness did not overcome it.

There was a man sent from God, whose name was John. He came as a witness to testify to the light, so that all might believe through him. He himself was not the light, but he came to testify to the light. The true light, which enlightens everyone, was coming into the world.

He was in the world, and the world came into being through him; yet the world did not know him. He came to what was his own, and his own people did not accept him. But to all who received him, who believed in his name, he gave power to become children of God, who were born, not of blood or of the will of the flesh or of the will of man, but of God.

And the Word became flesh and lived among us, and we have seen his glory, the glory as of a father's only son, full of grace and truth. (John testified to him and cried out, 'This is he of whom I said, "He who comes after me ranks ahead of me because he was before me."') From his fullness we have all received, grace upon grace. The law indeed was given through Moses; grace and truth came through Jesus Christ. No one has ever seen God. It is God the only Son, who is close to the Father's heart, who has made him known.

JOHN 1:1–18

Many years ago, when I was working in prison chaplaincy, a number of the men would gather in the chapel on a Friday evening to watch a *Fact and Faith* film. These films were made by an American father and son, both of whom were scientists and Christians. One in particular, lasting for about 15 minutes and with no soundtrack, burned itself on my memory. It consisted of shots of a young boy rowing himself across a lake on a bright summer's day. After a few minutes the picture froze, with the boy in mid-stroke. Then, slowly at first but gradually gathering speed, the camera moved outwards and upwards, showing us a bird's-eye view, then a plane's, then a rocket's—until the earth itself had become an insignificant dot, quickly lost within the myriad stars making up our Milky Way. Still the camera moved outwards, until the Milky Way itself was a vanishing speck among the other galaxies.

This journey into the outer reaches of the universe continued silently for about five minutes, and again the camera froze. The journey then replayed itself backwards until the camera zoomed in on the boy, this time focusing on a fly that had landed on his hand. After another momentary freeze, the journey into the fly's body began—past cells and platelets, onwards and ever inwards, until the inner universe of the fly's body resembled the outer universe that we had seen earlier, so closely that you couldn't tell the difference. After a final freezing of the picture came another return journey, bringing us back once more to the boy who serenely continued his journey across the lake.

The sheer magnitude of the creation makes us fearful, and, of all the four Gospels, John alone sets the events of Jesus' earthly life against the backdrop of cosmic prehistory. Each time we hear this reading—particularly at Christmas, as we celebrate the mystery of the incarnation—its awesome poetic rendering of the coming of the Word of God in human flesh fires our imaginations and sends tingles down the spine. Christian theology through the centuries has offered many reasons for the necessity of Jesus' human birth. Here is not the place to explore them all, but one such reason surely arose from God's compassionate recognition of our frailty and human limitations. Our hearts quail before the might, the majesty, the ungraspable vastness of God and his creation, and it should comfort us to know that we are not alone in this. The same emotions afflicted the psalmist: 'When I look at your heavens, the work of your fingers, the moon and the stars that you have established; what are human beings that you are mindful of them, mortals that you care for them?' (Psalm 8:3–4).

And so 'the Word became flesh and lived among us' (John 1:14). Faced with the seeming impossibility that we could in any way 'matter' to the Creator of the universe, we are invited to give our love and trust to his Son, who is able to sympathise with our weaknesses and 'who in every respect has been tempted as we are, yet without sin' (Hebrews 4:15). Knowing and experiencing the love of God for us in Christ gives us the courage to follow his lead into a deeper knowledge and awareness of him, a knowledge that ultimately transcends the limits of anything we can humanly express.

Our place in the infinite vastness of the cosmos confronts us this Lent with a particular form of 'desert' experience. We are invited to enter this desert with our hand firmly in the hand of Jesus, and to face the mind-boggling truth that we are, at the same time, both minute specks in an ever-evolving universe and persons who are deeply and irrevocably loved by God: 'I have loved you with an everlasting love' (Jeremiah 31:3). Jeremiah's affirmation and the following words of Diarmuid O'Murchu challenge us to respond to this paradoxical reality with courage, gratitude and a sense of wonder:

> *The divine is written all over creation: the quantum vacuum, the supernova explosions, the recurring cycle of birth–death–rebirth, the process of photosynthesis—these and many more are the chapters of our primary scriptures. Divinity abounds, in and around us.*[12]

For reflection and prayer

When I look at your heavens, the work of your fingers, the moon and the stars that you have established; what are human beings that you are mindful of them, mortals that you care for them?
PSALM 8:3–4

A question

Christians across the world and throughout history have been strengthened and inspired by an experience of Christ as Saviour and Friend. How comfortable are you with the 'cosmic Christ' of the prologue to John's Gospel, and how does this relate to the more intimate picture?

Week 2

Opening
the heart
in prayer

Sunday

'Lord, teach us to pray'

[Jesus] was praying in a certain place, and after he had finished, one of his disciples said to him, 'Lord, teach us to pray, as John taught his disciples.' He said to them, 'When you pray, say: Father, hallowed be your name. Your kingdom come. Give us each day our daily bread. And forgive us our sins, for we ourselves forgive everyone indebted to us. And do not bring us to the time of trial.'

LUKE 11:1–4

> *'Our Father…'*
> *'Yes?'*
> *'Don't interrupt me—I'm praying! Our Father…'*
> *'Yes, I'm here. You called me, and I'm very interested in what you have to say.'*

The passing of too many years to count have dimmed the memory of the exact wording, but I do remember a sketch that did the rounds of the churches and youth groups I was involved in, which began in this fashion. It was called 'Don't interrupt me—I'm praying!' and consisted of a conversation between a disciple who was trying to pray the Lord's Prayer and God the Father who insisted on 'interrupting' and answering every petition as it was spoken. It was cleverly written and very funny, but also intensely thought-provoking and challenging.

As we can see from the opening, it begins by making the point that, so often, we offer the words of our prayers without real thought or awareness. There is a danger that the very familiarity of the Lord's Prayer can lull us into a kind of 'sleepwalking' mentality in which we simply repeat the words mechanically, out of habit or a sense of duty. We mouth the words but our minds are elsewhere, or we are simply not attuned to the reality of a God who hears our prayers and may wish to speak to us in response. The disciple here has been caught out in this way: she is not really listening, so God's response is seen only as a tiresome interruption.

The version of the Lord's Prayer in today's reading is one of two: Matthew also records it, with slight variations (Matthew 6:9–13). In Matthew, 'Father' becomes 'Our Father in heaven', and the prayer that God's kingdom will come is followed by 'Your will be done, on earth as it is in heaven.' After the plea that God will keep us from the time of trial, Matthew's version concludes, 'but rescue us from the evil one.' Both versions offer corporate rather than individual petitions and speak consistently in the first person plural. The person praying prays inescapably as a member of the community of faith; there is no place here for ivory-towered isolation.

Luke lays more emphasis on Jesus' personal practice of prayer than does any other Gospel. We read elsewhere in Luke that the Spirit came upon Jesus while he was praying (3:21–22) and that he frequently withdrew to desert places to pray alone (5:16). He prayed always before significant moments in his ministry—for instance, the call of the disciples (6:12–13), the question about his identity (9:18) and the transfiguration (9:28). Later, as the pressure intensifies and the cross approaches, Luke records Jesus praying in Gethsemane (22:40–42), on the cross (23:34, 46) and, after his resurrection, at table with his disciples (24:30). Luke continues his emphasis on the importance of prayer in the book of Acts, where prayer is seen as the characteristic that distinguishes the communities of faith from the societies around them (Acts 1:14; 2:42; 12:12).

Both versions of the Lord's Prayer are placed by the authors within the context of extended passages of teaching on prayer and the life of discipleship (Luke 10:38—11:13; Matthew 5—7), again emphasising the truth that prayer is not an activity that takes place in isolation but one that takes place within the body of Christ and sustains and integrates the whole of life. One of the most challenging aspects about the sketch we began with was that, as the disciple worked through the prayer, God picked up each petition and applied it directly to the disciple's own life. So 'forgive us our sins' instantly became a question of the small misdemeanour that the disciple was trying to brush under the carpet; and 'for we ourselves forgive everyone indebted to us' threw the spotlight uncomfortably on a particular grudge the disciple had been nursing for a number of years.

If we have the courage to allow it, this prayer has the power to face us with the unpalatable reality of our own sin and weakness and to allow God's judging and healing light to shine into the darkest recesses of our human nature. We will no longer be simply saying the words out of habit, but will find ourselves deeply involved in God's healing and restoring work, both in ourselves and in the world around us. As the disciple in the sketch observes at one point, 'Lord, this is taking a lot longer than usual!'

The Lord's Prayer is far more than simply a prayer of petition. When the disciples ask Jesus how they should pray, he responds not by giving them a set of magic words but by revealing to them something of the nature of God as their heavenly Father. The prayer he gives them opens the heart and spirit to God and to the world, rather than closing them in on themselves. By inviting disciples to own their needs and weaknesses, the Lord's Prayer offers the possibility of real empathy with the needs and weakness of others.

It is surely when we become most acutely aware of our own need that we realise also our total dependency on God for our nourishment and sustenance, for the courage to face the truth about ourselves, for our need to forgive, and for our own forgiveness and healing. Beyond the simple prayer of petition, the Lord's Prayer has the potential to draw us beyond ourselves into the creative and contemplative life of the cosmos. We are deeply loved; we are not alone, and we are invited to play our part in God's work of healing in the world. We are unique and distinct beings, and we have been created by God to be an integral part of his creation—a work-in-progress of such hallowed beauty and wonder that it exceeds anything we can imagine.

For reflection and prayer
Likewise the Spirit helps us in our weakness; for we do not know how to pray as we ought, but that very Spirit intercedes with sighs too deep for words. And God, who searches the heart, knows what is the mind of the Spirit, because the Spirit intercedes for the saints according to the will of God.

ROMANS 8:26–27

A question

In what ways may the Lord's Prayer be able 'to draw us beyond ourselves into the creative and contemplative life of the cosmos'?

Singleness of heart

Now as they went on their way, he entered a certain village, where a woman named Martha welcomed him into her home. She had a sister named Mary, who sat at the Lord's feet and listened to what he was saying. But Martha was distracted by her many tasks; so she came to him and asked, 'Lord, do you not care that my sister has left me to do all the work by myself? Tell her then to help me.' But the Lord answered her, 'Martha, Martha, you are worried and distracted by many things; there is need of only one thing. Mary has chosen the better part, which will not be taken away from her.'

LUKE 10:38–42

From the time of the early Church Fathers, this incident in Jesus' life has been held up as an example of the tension between the 'active' and 'contemplative' lives in Christian discipleship and in our relationship with God. But Mary and Martha were not the first pairing to be allegorised in this way; both Philo[13] and Gregory the Great treat the Old Testament women Rachel and Leah in the same way (although they seem to disagree as to which quality each woman represents). Gregory expresses it thus: '... after the embrace of Leah, Jacob attains to Rachel, in that every one that is perfect is first joined to an active life in productiveness, and afterwards united to a contemplative life of rest.'[14]

The first person to use Martha and Mary as examples

of the active and contemplative lives seems to have been Origen (c.185–254), and this interpretation was taken up by Augustine: 'Martha chose a good part, but Mary the better. [Martha]… ministered to the hungry, the thirsty, the homeless: but all these pass away… "Mary hath chosen the better part, which shall not be taken away from her." She hath chosen to contemplate, to live by the Word.'[15]

This is fine as far as it goes, and contains more than an element of truth. In a church that continually stresses the importance of activity and visible and 'useful' involvement, this allegorical treatment of Mary and Martha highlights the vital role played by contemplation—the silent, single-minded focus on God that sustains all our living. Indeed, Jesus' assertion that Mary has chosen 'the better part' offers a robust challenge to our usual way of living and being, both as churches and as individuals.

And yet, I have never felt fully able to go along with this interpretation, feeling that it begs more questions than it answers. For instance, as we read of it in this account, is Martha's treatment by Jesus fair—or even courteous? Martha had welcomed Jesus into her home and was offering him generous hospitality, yet Jesus appeared to be belittling that offering by siding with her sister, who was doing nothing to help her. Was that really what Jesus was doing? And if so, what message has that sent out down the centuries to those countless numbers who have spent their lives in active work for others, both inside and outside the church?

Part of the problem has arisen from the fact that, originally, a life based on contemplative prayer was thought to be possible only for those living a religious life in a monastery or a convent. Only those dedicated in this way, it was believed, could live a Christian life that was 'perfect'. Those not called to such a life of prayer lived out their vocation as best they could in 'the world', with its many demands of home, family and work. But slowly, over time, this perspective began to change. When Benedict produced his Rule for monasteries in the sixth century, all the different aspects of the monastery's life were viewed as sacred, from serving at the altar to serving in the kitchen,[16] and by the 17th century the Carmelite lay brother Lawrence (1611–1691) was able to say, 'The time of business does not with me differ from the time of prayer; and in the noise and clutter of my kitchen… I possess God in as great tranquillity as if I were upon my knees before the Blessed Sacrament.'[17]

It is against this wider understanding of the relationship between active and contemplative living that the 20th-century Benedictine monk Thomas Keating treats the incident of Mary and Martha, and offers an intriguingly different inter-pretation.[18] In his view, the traditional understanding is too simplistic and doesn't adequately allow for the necessary work and activity with which most of us are inevitably involved. So he shifts the focus: for Keating, both Martha and Mary are engaged in activity, of different kinds but both equally valid. Where Mary is 'right' and Martha is 'wrong' is not in the activities themselves but in the attitude of heart of each woman while so engaged. The 'better part' chosen by Mary was her singleness of heart and purpose, while Martha's good work was undermined by her fretful resentment of Mary. The implication of Keating's view is that, had Martha been able to work with a similar singleness of heart (like Brother Lawrence), Jesus would have had no need to rebuke her.

There is good news here for all of us, whatever our parti-cular calling may be. Whatever our commitments and life experience, our activity offers the opportunity to 'practise the presence of God' in all that we do. But there is also a message of caution when we are tempted to judge a person's commitment to Christ by their level of visible activity and general 'usefulness'. In recent times, our churches have not had a good track record when it comes to understanding or even tolerating those whose vocation is solely to contemplative prayer—the calling simply to sit at Jesus' feet, as Mary did, and listen to him. If and when this is our reaction, we need to take the meaning of Jesus' words to Martha to heart: 'Leave Mary alone! This is the work I have given her to do!'

For reflection and prayer
Rejoice in the Lord always... Let your gentleness be known to everyone. The Lord is near. Do not worry about anything, but in everything by prayer and supplication with thanksgiving let your requests be made known to God. And the peace of God, which surpasses all understanding, will guard your hearts and your minds in Christ Jesus.

PHILIPPIANS 4:4–7 (ABRIDGED)

A question
'The time of business does not with me differ from the time of prayer; and in the noise and clutter of my kitchen... I possess God in as great tranquillity as if I were upon my knees before the Blessed Sacrament.' How might these words of Brother Lawrence help us bring singleness of heart and purpose to all that we do?

Tuesday

Where can I flee from your presence?

Now the word of the Lord came to Jonah son of Amittai, saying, 'Go at once to Nineveh, that great city, and cry out against it; for their wickedness has come before me.' But Jonah set out to flee to Tarshish from the presence of the Lord.

JONAH 1:1–3a

The author of the book of Jonah seems to have his tongue planted firmly in his cheek when he introduces his hero as 'Jonah son of Amittai'. The literal meaning of the name is 'dove, son of faithfulness', and, as the writer immediately makes clear, Jonah is anything but faithful. God's call to him is uncompromising, ordering Jonah to go instantly to Nineveh to proclaim God's judgment against the city. Jonah does not argue verbally but instead votes with his feet, immediately boarding a ship sailing in the opposite direction, to Tarshish.

It is not clear whether Jonah genuinely fears God with his sovereign authority (perhaps in the manner of the servant who buried his single talent in the ground because he knew his master to be a harsh man, reaping where he had not sown: Matthew 25:24–25), whether he doubts his own ability to fulfil the task, fearing ridicule or failure (like Moses in Exodus 3:13; 4:1, 10, and the prophet in Jeremiah 1:6), or whether he simply wants the freedom to live his life according to his own whims and desires, untroubled and uncomplicated by the divine command. Whatever the root causes of Jonah's resistance, the outcome is the same: he attempts to run away from God as fast as he can. It is a reaction that would clearly have resonated with the late 19th-century English poet, Francis Thompson:

> *I fled him, down the nights and down the days;*
> *I fled him, down the arches of the years;*
> *I fled him, down the labyrinthine ways*
> *Of my own mind; and in the midst of tears*
> *I hid from him...*
> *From those strong Feet that followed, followed after.*

So begins Thompson's celebrated poem 'The hound of heaven'.[19] Thompson was a devout Roman Catholic who led a tortured life. After abortive attempts to become first a priest and then a doctor, he fell into extreme poverty; he earned a little money by selling matches but had to borrow paper on which to write his poetry. His health was not good and, in order to relieve the pain of acute neuralgia, he began taking the opium-based drug laudanum. This led to addiction, and his health never fully recovered. He died of TB just before his 48th birthday.

The image Thompson uses to evoke the character of God in this poem is initially a terrifying one: God is the 'hound of heaven' who relentlessly and remorselessly tracks down his prey. It is an image that has resonated with those whose experience of God is one of arbitrary, unfeeling power. Yet, despite the graphic violence of the imagery he employs, we are soon given a hint that Thompson is well aware of a deeper dimension than simple tyranny to God's motive in pursuing him. He interrupts his narrative to confess, using brackets:

(For, though I knew His love Who followed,
Yet was I sore adread
Lest having Him, I must have naught beside.)

Here, we may feel, is the crux of the matter: if Thompson submits, he fears the loss of everything he holds dear. As the poem draws to its close, however, he comes to realise that it is not for reasons of personal power or wrathful vengeance that God pursues him so relentlessly, but because of a profound and eternal love in which all that the seeker most deeply longs for will be discovered in all its fullness:

'All which I took from thee I did but take,
Not for thy harms.
But just that thou might'st seek it in my arms.
All which thy child's mistake
Fancies as lost, I have stored for thee at home;
Rise, clasp My hand, and come!'

We may appreciate only too well some aspects of the reluctance of both Jonah and Francis Thompson when it comes to responding to the call of God in our lives. The words of Matthew 6:33 ('But strive first for the kingdom of God and his righteousness, and all these things will be given to you as well') trip readily enough off our tongues, but most of us find it far more difficult to live the truth they express. Our lifelong journey of faith offers us the gift of a gradual growth into this truth—that all we most love, cherish and deeply long for will find its ultimate fulfilment in the rich mystery that is the everlasting love of God for each one of us in Christ.

A major waymark on our journey comes when we begin to realise that the God who calls us to be his own accompanies us and shields us every step of the way. It begins to dawn on us, with a sense of wondering gratitude, that he really does accept us as we are and, with gentle insistence, compels us to allow him to love us. We have already seen one lovely expression of this reality in George Herbert's poem, 'Love (III)'. In our deepening relationship with God in Christ, we may find the boundaries of our prayer gradually expanding. No longer is it one (important) activity among many to be fitted into our busy days; it has been transmuted into the spiritual air we breathe, as vital to our souls as oxygen to our bodies. Like Jonah and Francis Thompson, we too are invited to allow God to use our life experience as the raw material within which his love can act, so that we may come to know that nothing 'in all creation will be able to separate us from the love of God in Christ Jesus our Lord' (Romans 8:39).

For reflection and prayer

Where can I go from your spirit? Or where can I flee from your presence? If I ascend to heaven, you are there; if I make my bed in Sheol, you are there. If I take the wings of the morning and settle at the farthest limits of the sea, even there your hand shall lead me, and your right hand shall hold me fast.

PSALM 139:7–10

A question

Are you able to identify specific times in your own life when you know you have been fleeing from 'the hound of heaven'?

Wednesday

Out of the depths

They went to a place called Gethsemane; and he said to his disciples, 'Sit here while I pray.' He took with him Peter and James and John, and began to be distressed and agitated. And he said to them, 'I am deeply grieved, even to death; remain here, and keep awake.' And going a little farther, he threw himself on the ground and prayed that, if it were possible, the hour might pass from him. He said, 'Abba, Father, for you all things are possible; remove this cup from me; yet, not what I want, but what you want.' He came and found them sleeping; and he said to Peter, 'Simon, are you asleep? Could you not keep awake for one hour? Keep awake and pray that you may not come into the time of trial; the spirit indeed is willing, but the flesh is weak.' And again he went away and prayed, saying the same words. And once more he came and found them sleeping, for their eyes were very heavy; and they did not know what to say to him. He came a third time and said to them, 'Are you still sleeping and taking your rest? Enough! The hour has come; the Son of Man is betrayed into the hands of sinners. Get up, let us be going. See, my betrayer is at hand.'

MARK 14:32–42

We know from elsewhere in the Gospels that there were occasions when Jesus prayed in the presence of his disciples (Luke 11:1), so it may well be that, to begin with, this time seemed no different from many others. Having instructed his disciples to sit and wait for him, he took his 'inner circle' of Peter, James and John to witness his prayer at closer quarters. This was not the first time that this inner group had been so privileged: Jesus had previously taken them with him when he restored Jairus' daughter to life (Mark 5:37) and when he had been transfigured on the mountain (9:2). It is likely that Mark intends his readers to remember the transfiguration experience, when these same disciples witnessed Jesus' prayer to his Father in the presence of Moses and Elijah. All three disciples had asserted the intensity and depth of their commitment to Jesus: Peter had rashly claimed to be prepared to follow him to death if necessary (John 13:37; Mark 14:29), and James and John had stated their willingness to drink the same cup as Jesus was to drink (Matthew 20:22)—in other words, that they were ready to die for him.

On the eve of his crucifixion, then, Jesus takes Peter, James and John with him, instructs them to stay awake and chooses to allow them to witness the depth of his anguish. The NIV seems to muffle the intensity of Jesus' emotions, using terms such as 'sorrow' and 'troubled' rather than 'grieved' and 'agitated', as in the NRSV translation, which accentuates the acute rawness of Jesus' pain. The Gethsemane account in Luke 22:39–46 intensifies the agony by including a verse absent from some of the ancient manuscripts: 'In his anguish he prayed more earnestly, and his sweat became like great drops of blood falling down on the ground' (v. 44). It is as if Jesus deliberately planned to give his inner circle a foretaste of the reality for which they had so rashly and thoughtlessly asked.

The warning to 'keep awake' (Mark 14:34, 38) would surely have had levels of resonance both for the disciples themselves and for Mark's readers. On the simplest level, there was clearly the question of simple human need: Jesus knew only too well that the crisis was almost upon him and, in the extremity of his distress, he did not want to be left alone. At a deeper level, the injunction to keep awake will have signalled the imminence of Jesus' 'hour' and the need for everyone to be watchful and ready. This theme formed a growing thread in Israel's later history (Psalm 130:6; Sirach 4:20 in the Old Testament Apocrypha) and is picked up repeatedly by Jesus in his teaching. Parables such as that of the wise and foolish bridesmaids (Matthew 25:1–13) and the rich farmer (Luke 12:16–21) illustrate graphically the dire consequences for those who are not awake and ready. So Jesus' words to his disciples echo an apocalyptic warning (Matthew 24:42). Often, until this point, Jesus has sounded a note of restraint, saying that his hour has not yet come, but now the time of testing is upon them and the climactic event of Jesus' 'hour'—his death and resurrection—is imminent.

Out of many possible strands for our reflection, perhaps we may concentrate particularly on one. We may find ourselves in some sympathy with the disciples: how do you accompany someone who is suffering as deeply as Jesus was, especially if it is someone you love? We may well have experienced for ourselves just how hard it is to sit with somebody who is in pain, knowing that there is nothing we can do to take it away. People who have been bereaved often speak of others crossing the road in order to avoid speaking to them. Such insensitivity, usually caused by the other person's own distress and sense of helplessness rather than any desire to hurt, compound the suffering of the one bereaved. It would not have been surprising if the disciples experienced the same difficulty. Quite apart from the lateness of the hour and the general tension of the occasion, it is possible that their falling asleep functioned as a sort of psychological 'crossing the road'. Jesus had asked them to remain with him and, physically, they did; but, finding his pain too much to bear, their falling asleep also functioned as a simple safety valve.

When I was beginning my training as a counsellor, one of the first and hardest things to learn was the need simply to sit and listen to the other person, without either trying to 'put things right' or imposing my own view of the way things should be. It is a lesson that Jesus had repeatedly attempted to teach the disciples, on one occasion delivering a sharp rebuke to Peter (Matthew 16:23; see Week 4, Tuesday) and on another giving a general reprimand to all the disciples (Mark 10:13–14). Simply to accept the other person, allowing things to be the way they are without attempting to lighten the load artificially, will be the most precious gift we can give.

For reflection and prayer

Out of the depths I cry to you, O Lord. Lord, hear my voice! ... I wait for the Lord, my soul waits, and in his word I hope; my soul waits for the Lord more than those who watch for the morning.

PSALM 130:1–2, 5–6 (ABRIDGED)

A question

How do we stay alongside a person in acute anguish, while at the same time recognising our own helplessness and inability to 'put the situation right'?

Ask, and it will be given you

'Do not judge, so that you may not be judged. For with the judgment you make you will be judged, and the measure you give will be the measure you get... Do not give what is holy to dogs; and do not throw your pearls before swine, or they will trample them under foot and turn and maul you. Ask, and it will be given to you; search, and you will find; knock, and the door will be opened for you. For everyone who asks receives, and everyone who searches finds, and for everyone who knocks, the door will be opened. Is there anyone among you who, if your child asks for bread, will give a stone? Or if the child asks for a fish, will give a snake? If you then, who are evil, know how to give good gifts to your children, how much more will your Father in heaven give good things to those who ask him!'

MATTHEW 7:1–2, 6–11

We spent some time yesterday reflecting on the behaviour of Peter, James and John when Jesus asked them to wait with him in Gethsemane while he prayed. We did not then focus on the content of Jesus' prayer itself, but we do so today within the context of Jesus' own teaching on asking things of God in prayer: 'Ask... search... knock... For everyone who asks receives...' (vv. 7–8). As Jesus sees his inevitable death approaching, in the intensity of his distress he prays that, if it is possible, his Father would 'remove this cup' from him. 'Yet,' he adds, 'not what I want, but what you want' (Mark 14:36). How does Jesus' earlier teaching on prayer square with his agonised plea that his Father would make another way, other than the cross, possible?

'If it be the Lord's will...' I have known a number of Christians over the years who have viewed this addition to prayers of intercession as something of a cop-out, as if it indicated a lack of faith and trust on the part of the person praying. Indeed, a superficial reading of the part of today's text that refers to asking for things in prayer could seem to affirm that view. Fathers will not give their children a stone when they ask for bread, so why believe that God would not give his beloved children what they ask for? Ask, and you will receive—it's as simple as that. Yet all, surely, is not quite as it first appears.

Two particular points may give us some assistance here. The first lies in Jesus' intention when adding the 'not what I want...' caveat to his prayer. Far from being a cop-out, this indicated a profound recognition that the aims and purposes of God extended far beyond the crisis of the present moment. Despite his anguish, Jesus was aware of that, and offered his prayer within that context. Secondly, we may be helped by looking at the context in which the Gospel writer has set this teaching. Our passage opens, 'Do not judge, so that you may not be judged', and the uncomfortably graphic illustration of logs in our own eyes and specks in our neighbours' exposes our habitual blindness when it comes to awareness of our own sin. This is followed by the injunction not to give what is holy to dogs or throw pearls before swine, which seems to counsel us not to squander what is sacred on those who would denigrate and ridicule it.

Much of the teaching in this passage resonates with the proverbial wisdom of ancient Hebrew tradition, but Jesus' prophetic proclamation of the kingdom gives it an added twist. In this context it is not simply good advice, but, at a deeper level, demonstrates the radical demands of committed discipleship. 'Ask... seek... knock...' On one level, it *is* simple: we are urged to come to God with our requests, with the transparency and simplicity of a child approaching a deeply loved father. But the context of that relationship is vital: 'Prayer is a quest and an expectation,' says Eugene Boring,[20] and is based on a growing and deepening relationship. Without that relationship, our prayers are nothing more than a shopping list of requests.

The instruction not to judge, similarly, is inseparable from the context of relationship with our God. What does it mean? Through history, the church has had difficulty in coming to terms with these words, always struggling with the temptation to rationalise them or to water down their uncompromising demands. Clearly, we are expected to use our judgment in the context of discerning right from wrong and in determining appropriate behaviour. What Jesus is absolutely set against is the all-too-human tendency (even for disciples) to backbite, compete against each other, undermine and condemn, to judge on the basis of a partial knowledge and to draw wrong and damaging conclusions on the basis of that limited awareness. Harmful though such behaviour always is, however, Jesus is not primarily concerned with successful strategies for good relationships in the world, but rather with a call 'to live in the light of the dawning kingdom of God'.[21]

When we pray for others, obviously the presenting need

will be uppermost in our minds. As children of the kingdom, though, our inner eyes will need also to be on the distant horizon, acknowledging the unseen presence of the wider picture of God's plans and purposes. Jesus' teaching here brings us back full circle, acting as a form of commentary on petitions in the Lord's Prayer: 'Your kingdom come. Your will be done, on earth as it is in heaven' (Matthew 6:10). When we pray these words, we are asking God to enable us to see with his eyes and to tune our own desires and will more closely to his own. We seek to grow in acceptance of the radical discipleship call that these words represent—the decision to move away from the prevailing cultural values of our time, into a life of deepening trust and obedience.

For reflection and prayer
To set the mind on the flesh is death, but to set the mind on the Spirit is life and peace.
ROMANS 8:6

Let the same mind be in you that was in Christ Jesus.
PHILIPPIANS 2:5

A question
How do you see Jesus' injunction not to judge working out in your own life? Can you think of situations that might need some work and prayer in this area?

Praying with the imagination

Now all the tax-collectors and sinners were coming near to listen to [Jesus]. And the Pharisees and the scribes were grumbling and saying, 'This fellow welcomes sinners and eats with them.' So he told them this parable: 'Which one of you, having a hundred sheep and losing one of them, does not leave the ninety-nine in the wilderness and go after the one that is lost until he finds it? When he has found it, he lays it on his shoulders and rejoices. And when he comes home, he calls together his friends and neighbours, saying to them, "Rejoice with me, for I have found my sheep that was lost." Just so, I tell you, there will be more joy in heaven over one sinner who repents than over ninety-nine righteous people who need no repentance.'

LUKE 15:1–7

When I was around nine or ten years old, one comment appeared with monotonous regularity on my school reports: 'Could do better: she spends far too much of her time daydreaming.' I loved writing, and during that period stories of all kinds poured from my pen; but as time went on, I sensed that, while writing stories was all very well, there was an increasing expectation that I should be starting to concentrate on more 'serious' work.

In the Christian tradition, the use of the imagination on the spiritual journey has had a chequered history and experienced a parallel ambivalence to that in my own life. For some Christians, there remains a lurking suspicion that 'imagination' equates to something 'fanciful' or 'not true'— or even something perverse and downright wrong. Certain scriptures declaring that false prophets 'prophesy out of their own imagination' (Ezekiel 13:2) and that images of false gods have been 'formed by the art and imagination of mortals' (Acts 17:29) have increased this uneasiness.

Yet the approach that Jesus took should surely banish this misunderstanding for good. Today's reading offers an example of his preferred method of teaching—the parable. In parables, he repeatedly appealed to his hearers' imaginations. And how did he do this? By using what was to hand—the stuff of creation and the raw materials and situations of people's everyday lives. Often he would precede the parable with an injunction to *listen*: listen to the words; allow them to paint a vivid picture in your mind; let the reality and truth of that picture draw you deeper into the love and wisdom that is God. And the images and word-pictures poured from him: 'You are the salt of the earth… You are the light of the world' (Matthew 5:13–14); 'A sower went out to sow his seed' (Luke 8:5); the kingdom of God is 'like a mustard seed' (Mark 4:31), 'like treasure hidden in a field' (Matthew 13:44), 'like a net that was thrown into the sea and caught fish of every kind' (v. 47). And as the supreme parable, he gave the people the icon of himself: 'I am the bread of life' (John 6:35); 'I am the light of the world' (9:5); 'I am the good shepherd' (10:11); 'I am the way, and the truth, and the life' (14:6).

This appeal to the imagination was taken up powerfully

by the 16th-century spiritual master Ignatius Loyola, whose Spiritual Exercises have had such a profound influence on the lives of so many Christians today. Baptised originally as Inigo (later taking the name Ignacio) de Oñaz y Loyola, he was born around the year 1491, the son of a wealthy and aristocratic family. Originally intended for the church, he soon abandoned this idea in favour of a life at court and in the army.

On 20 May 1521, while leading the military defence of Pamplona in Navarre, Ignatius was severely wounded. It was during his convalescence that he experienced a profound religious conversion, which turned him from a soldier fighting for his country to one seeking to follow Christ with his whole being. One particular experience was pivotal to his change of heart. As a young man, Ignatius had always enjoyed tales of valour and chivalry, and had been stirred and energised by his reading. The place where he was convalescing had no reading material of this type; only a Life of Christ and a collection of saints' lives were available. As he began to read, Ignatius realised that he was alternating between two types of imaginative daydreaming. The first was inspired by the impressive military feats he would achieve and the great lady whose love he would win when he had recovered; the second, to his surprise, began to emerge from his religious reading. He initially indulged in both types of daydream, but gradually, a difference emerged. It was a difference that would not only radically change his own life-direction but would influence the lives of many millions of others.

Ignatius' discovery was that, while both types of daydream were enjoyable at the time, the dreams of chivalry ultimately left him feeling bored, restless and empty, but those inspired by his religious reading left him happy, hopeful and greatly encouraged. Consequently, when he came to compile the Spiritual Exercises, the work of prayerful imagination became central to the experience of those journeying through them.

People following the Ignatian path today are encouraged to engage in an imaginative form of Gospel contemplation, picturing themselves present in a Gospel scene, looking on with the bystanders or identifying with the key participants. It is not for everybody but, for those drawn down this spiritual path, the activity has the potential to be far more than daydreaming. The writer Fran Herder has commented that our lives unfold in a sequence of stories, and that the particular pull that Bible stories of all sorts have for us lies in the fact that the issues they deal with are timeless. We all have the experience of being born, being lost and being fed. We have all known experiences of learning, and know what it is to suffer. We read the stories in the Bible and find 'that they move us, challenge us, and evoke recognition in our hearts... the scriptures we call *sacred* draw us in, inviting us to spend time, entering them deeply enough to be transformed'.[22]

For reflection and prayer

'I will open my mouth to speak in parables; I will proclaim what has been hidden from the foundation of the world.'
MATTHEW 13:35

'But blessed are your eyes, for they see, and your ears, for they hear.'
MATTHEW 13:16

A question

What part does imagination play in your own spiritual life? Do you expect God to speak to you in and through your hopes, dreams and desires?

Saturday

A little word

'When you are praying, do not heap up empty phrases as the Gentiles do; for they think that they will be heard because of their many words. Do not be like them, for your Father knows what you need before you ask him.'

MATTHEW 6:7–8

These two short verses form part of an extended passage expressing Jesus' teaching on prayer, some aspects of which we have already considered this week (Thursday). Jesus has been criticising hypocritical prayer in the synagogue (6:5–6), but here he extends this criticism to warped Gentile practice. He is not concerned here with good and noble examples of Gentile prayer but with those who seek to batter the deity with their many words. Jesus' concern seems to be operating on two levels—the first aimed at resisting the temptation to pile up unnecessary words, because 'your Father knows what you need before you ask him', and the second, more seriously, stressing the need to avoid using words as a manipulative tool. Behind Jesus' teaching may lie the practice of the Gentiles in the invocation of many gods, and in their use of elaborately correct formulae, hoping to ensure the 'effectiveness' of the prayer in satisfying the agenda of the one who was praying.

From its earliest beginnings, the church took Jesus' warning seriously. It began to develop a prayerful approach to the reading of scripture (*meditatio*), through which the inner meaning of the text was gradually interiorised. This formed part of the wider scheme known as *lectio divina*, which involved the prayerful repetition of the chosen text, first aloud, then silently in the mind, and finally absorbed into the depths of the heart. This is a very different approach to scripture from the one we were considering yesterday. Then, we were reflecting on the role our imaginations could usefully play in prayer; here, we are engaging in a process of 'spiritual digestion' as our soul feeds on the spiritual food of scripture. This method of scriptural prayer was the source of the ferment of the theological creativity of the early Christian centuries, particularly in the Fathers and Mothers of the desert tradition and the work of John Cassian, whom we first met on Thursday of Week 1.

In his Tenth Conference, entitled 'On Prayer',[23] Cassian describes this method of meditation, which he claimed was already ancient tradition by the fourth century, and was a method of such radical simplicity that it could be accessible to anyone, whether literate or not. The focus was on a small portion of scripture ('Be pleased, O God, to deliver me. O Lord, make haste to help me', Psalm 70:1), which was to be repeated constantly and would lead to a genuine poverty of spirit, in which there was a complete renunciation of 'the whole wealth and abundance of thoughts'.[24]

A further development of the teaching subsequently reduced the scripture verse to a single word, and it is this form of the teaching that is advocated by the anonymous author of *The Cloud of Unknowing* in the 14th century. The author urges that, in order to keep things as simple as possible, the word chosen for meditation should be of just one syllable, such as 'God', 'Love' or 'Peace'. He continues, 'Choose which one you prefer, or any other according to your liking—the word of one syllable that you like best. Fasten this word to your heart, so that whatever happens, it will never go away.'[25]

Initially, this teaching was available only to those living the religious life in monasteries or convents, but in our own time it has become available to all. This has been largely due to the work of two Benedictine monks, John Main and Thomas Keating, who have each adapted the teaching of *The Cloud of Unknowing* in slightly different ways for contemporary disciples. John Main's approach takes a specific, four-syllable word (Maranatha: 'Come, Lord Jesus') and instructs those praying to use it as a mantra, repeating it over and over on the lips, in the mind and finally in the heart. This approach to the prayer word has helped many thousands of Christians, and the World Community for Christian Meditation (www.wccm.org) continues to promote this teaching.

Thomas Keating also takes the teaching on the prayer word from *The Cloud* as his starting point but treats it somewhat differently. He is less prescriptive than John Main and follows *The Cloud* in encouraging the disciple to choose their own prayer-word, of preferably one syllable. Keating calls his approach 'centring prayer', and suggests that the disciple, rather than repeating the word as a mantra, 'gently place it in your awareness each time you recognise you are thinking about some other thought'.[26] The sacred word is not to be thought of as a magic wand and should not be viewed as the means of suppressing all thoughts, which is impossible. It rather 'directs your intention towards God and thus fosters a favourable atmosphere for the development of the deeper awareness to which your spiritual nature is attracted'.[27] It is a way of saying to God, 'Here I am'—and the next step is up to God. Many people have experienced a deepening and enrichment of their prayer by following this approach, and the worldwide organisation Contemplative Outreach continues Keating's work.[28]

Whichever form of prayer-word practice we may find attractive, the implications are the same. As John Cassian indicated back in the fourth century, we are being invited to welcome an aspect of voluntary poverty, where we consciously and deliberately try to resist the temptation to cushion ourselves protectively with many words when we approach God in prayer. Unconsciously we fear exposure to his truth, and we use words as a form of protective armour. It is as if we are saying, 'Thus far, and no further', because we know that we fear what uncomfortable truths we may be shown and what God may ask of us. The prayer-word offers a means of gently challenging our resistance, enabling God to bring healing and wholeness to our hearts and lives.

For reflection and prayer

With my whole heart I seek you; do not let me stray from your commandments. I treasure your word in my heart, so that I may not sin against you... I will delight in your statutes; I will not forget your word.

PSALM 119:10–11, 16

A question

Jesus warned his disciples not to 'heap up empty phrases' (Matthew 6:7) when they prayed. How 'wordy' are our prayers? How comfortable are we with restricting ourselves to a 'prayer word' as the basis for our prayer?

Week 3

Oases of welcome

Created glory

You make springs gush forth in the valleys; they flow between the hills, giving drink to every wild animal; the wild asses quench their thirst. By the streams the birds of the air have their habitation; they sing among the branches... You cause the grass to grow for the cattle, and plants for people to use, to bring forth food from the earth, and wine to gladden the human heart, oil to make the face shine, and bread to strengthen the human heart. The trees of the Lord are watered abundantly... In them the birds build their nests; the stork has its home in the fir trees... You have made the moon to mark the seasons; the sun knows its time for setting. You make darkness, and it is night, when all the animals of the forest come creeping out. The young lions roar for their prey, seeking their food from God. When the sun rises, they withdraw and lie down in their dens. People go out to their work and to their labour until the evening.

PSALM 104:10–23 (ABRIDGED)

The twelfth-century German Benedictine nun Hildegard of Bingen was one of the most remarkable women of the Middle Ages. Theologian and visionary, poet and mystic, naturalist and healer, musician and (some believe) artist, she gained the attention and respect of the political and religious leaders of her day. Many of her visions were later illustrated and one of the most striking is entitled 'The cycle of life'.[29] Here, we are confronted by a cosmic wheel, sustained by the God of creation, rotating in the vastness of space. The skill of the artist has succeeded in conveying the natural elements in all their forms—heat and cold, the growing and dying of the light, the rich spectrum of colour, and that fundamental 'greenness' (*viriditas*, a favourite theme of Hildegard's) which underlies all of creation's life and vitality. The circle that forms the inner hub of this wheel is subdivided into four coloured quarters representing the different seasons of the year. Above each section, trees radiate from the hub, each reflecting the growth, flourishing and dying that are the seasons' characteristics.

The German scholar Heinrich Schipperges describes the ferment of activity depicted on the surface of the wheel's hub, where 'the rich visual imagery... displays the very pulse of life as bound up with the practical sequence of seasonal tasks: trees are felled, the ground is prepared, and ripe fruit is gathered. Game is hunted, hay is taken in, corn is cut, and the harvest is brought home. Then people rest and celebrate.'[30]

Hildegard's graphic vision could be seen as providing a vivid visual commentary on the psalm from which today's passage is taken. Here, too, we are given a sense of a cosmic wheel, with God himself, 'wrapped with light as with a garment' (Psalm 104:2), central to the whole creative process. The word-picture conveys a sense of beauty, order and harmony; the four ancient elements of earth (v. 5), air (v. 3), fire (v. 4) and water (vv. 3, 6, 10–13) are all present. Each aspect of the creation—including humanity—unfolds, blessing God and being blessed in return by the simple act of taking its natural place within an ecosystem that is healthy and flourishing. We have space here for only a short extract, but the whole psalm repays close attention.

The awe-inspiring majesty of God as reflected in his creation is certainly biblical, but the Bible has little to say about the natural world as we tend to be drawn to it today—as a place of beauty, rest and refreshment away from the world of industry, commerce and overcrowded cities. The theologian David Brown has commented that our more idealised view of nature as an aid to escapism developed with the Romantic movement of the late 18th and early 19th centuries.

To earlier generations Switzerland or the Lake District were most likely to conjure up purely negative images, of forbidding threat or fear, and indeed to retreat into such places was often seen as the northern equivalent of moving into the desert, a place where demons had to be fought and overcome.[31]

This was certainly true of the Celtic monks of the sixth to eighth centuries, who often settled, as small communities or solitaries, on islands such as Iona, Lindisfarne or Bardsey Island off the coast of North Wales. A cluster of the monks' beehive huts clings perilously to the summit of the vertiginous island Skellig Michael, eight miles off the coast of County Kerry in the Atlantic ocean. People in the Celtic period and before removed themselves to these remote areas not to admire the beauty of the landscape but to deepen their relationship with God, and to test their commitment under the most demanding of physical conditions.

In today's society, the greed and over-consumption in recent decades have done much to destroy the sense of order and harmony so eloquently described in Psalm 104. It was not always so. I remember being taught about crop rotation when I was at school: a field would be sown with a different crop over three successive years, each of which would make varying demands on the soil. The field was then left fallow for a fourth year, enabling the soil to rest and nutrients to be re-established before the whole cycle began again. But with the advent of intensive farming methods and the pressure to squeeze every last bit of profit from the soil, the 'resting' phase of the cycle is often overlooked today. With this omission, an important element in the soil's natural rhythm and the restoration of balance is compromised.

In Genesis 1, God created humankind in his image and gave them dominion 'over every living thing'. Humanity's present thoughtless exploitation of the earth's resources reflects our global amnesia regarding the first part of that equation. We are called to reflect the image of God planted deep within us, and Psalm 104 challenges us to renew our commitment to cooperate with him in working for the restoration of beauty, order and harmony in our troubled world.

For reflection and prayer

So God created humankind in his image... and God said to them, 'Be fruitful and multiply, and fill the earth and subdue it; and have dominion... over every living thing that moves upon the earth.'

GENESIS 1:27–28 (ABRIDGED)

A question

Ponder the shape and content of your present life pattern. Is the balance of elements you find there weighted more towards domination or towards stewardship and cooperation?

The tree of life

And the Lord God planted a garden in Eden, in the east; and there he put the man whom he had formed. Out of the ground the Lord God made to grow every tree that is pleasant to the sight and good for food, the tree of life also in the midst of the garden, and the tree of the knowledge of good and evil.

GENESIS 2:8–9

Then the angel showed me the river of the water of life, bright as crystal, flowing from the throne of God and of the Lamb through the middle of the street of the city. On either side of the river is the tree of life with its twelve kinds of fruit, producing its fruit each month; and the leaves of the tree are for the healing of the nations.

REVELATION 22:1–2

A few minutes' walk away from where I live, there is a small, relatively traffic-free country lane that has so far miraculously escaped the attentions of the developer. It is a place of great beauty and peace, fringed by wood and common land, winding uphill and down on its gentle progress towards the local village. At the top of the lane lies a field edged on its southern boundary by a line of six immense oak trees, broad of girth and reach, towering 60 or 70 feet into the sky. The last two in the line have taken root slightly too close to one another; over time, the one on the extreme right has graciously leaned outwards, allowing breathing and growing space for her sister. Both have flourished. Whether distilling the dappled sunlight through their leaves in the crystalline stillness of the early morning or rending the ear as a howling gale tears through their yielding branches, they speak to the human spirit of the gratuitous, awe-inspiring beauty of God's creation, and of peace and reassurance in the midst of the ever-revolving cycle of life. The writer Eva Heymann is a member of the Society of the Holy Child Jesus, and she writes of trees as her friends, teachers and healers.

They were the first created beings in whom I could place my trust: trees heard me—not with ears like people, but as silent beings who were never too busy to listen. I felt at home with them—and shared my joys and sorrows with them. There was a real sense of being in relationship not only with trees, but with the whole of nature in all its manifold wonder.[32]

Trees are, and always have been, far more than simply majestic and awe-inspiring examples of God's creative power. Eva Heymann speaks for herself but echoes the experience of many others when she describes trees as embodying the life-giving properties of healing and wisdom. Academic opinion may be divided as to whether the tree of life and the tree of the knowledge of good and evil in our Genesis reading refer to one tree or two, but for our purposes the question is not important. Either way, the powerful symbol of the tree of life, featured in both Genesis and Revelation, embraces the entire biblical text like a pair of bookends.

Quite apart from its significance in the Bible, the tree of life has proved to be a powerful and significant symbol across a whole range of religions and mythologies. In pre-Christian

Norse literature,[33] the immense ash tree known as *Yggdrasil* (Odin's horse) is central to Scandinavian mythology and religion. It is the daily gathering place of the gods; creatures of various kinds live within it; its roots extend deep below the earth and its branches reach far into the heavens. Many other nations and faiths testify to a tree of life within their culture and folklore, Egypt, China and Armenia among them. In Egyptian mythology, the Holy Sycamore stood on the threshold between life and death—a meaning perhaps echoed (or anticipated?) by the nature and function of the tree(s) in the biblical garden of Eden. Similarly, the Tree of Life in Chinese tradition produces fruit that bestows immortality on the one who eats it.

The hauntingly beautiful ninth-century poem 'The dream of the rood'[34] integrates many of these pre-Christian and Christian themes. The poem has come down to us in two forms, one as a full-length poem and the other as extracts from an earlier version of the poem, which have been carved on the eighth-century Ruthwell Cross.[35] The theme of the poem is the triumph of the cross on which Christ died, and it unites images from heroic poetry, liturgical material and contemplative prayer. Its unique approach is that the voice of the poem is given to the rood (the cross) itself, which tells its story from its beginnings as a tree growing on the edge of the forest, its felling, and its destiny to become the cross on which Christ died. This 'noble tree' towers up to the sky, sometimes bloodstained, sometimes adorned with gold, jewels and precious hangings. The style of the writing is heroic, reminiscent of the slightly earlier Old English poem 'Beowulf'. But the image of the tree, running like a thread throughout, succeeds in recalling not only the tree of Christ's cross but also the tree in the Genesis garden and Revelation's tree with healing leaves, planted astride the river of life in the heavenly Jerusalem.

We have travelled some way from the oak trees fringing the country lane near my home, but, on whatever level we view them, trees have the capacity to nourish and sustain us, offering an oasis for our bruised souls. To return to the words of Eva Heymann:

> *My roots are deep in eternity.*
> *I grow beyond myself and sing*
> *With the wind*
> *The eternal song of love.*
> *I shelter and listen to all*
> *Who touch my mystery.*[36]

For reflection and prayer

Happy are those who find wisdom, and those who get understanding... She is a tree of life to those who lay hold of her; those who hold her fast are called happy.

PROVERBS 3:13, 18

'You will know them by their fruits. Are grapes gathered from thorns, or figs from thistles? In the same way, every good tree bears good fruit, but the bad tree bears bad fruit.'

MATTHEW 7:16–17

A question

Throughout history, trees have been powerful symbols of life, wisdom and continuity. What wisdom can you glean from the trees in your neighbourhood?

Tuesday

Pilgrimage

How lovely is your dwelling-place, O Lord of hosts! My soul longs, indeed it faints for the courts of the Lord; my heart and my flesh sing for joy to the living God... Happy are those whose strength is in you, in whose heart are the highways to Zion. As they go through the valley of Baca they make it a place of springs; the early rain also covers it with pools. They go from strength to strength; the God of gods will be seen in Zion.

PSALM 84:1–2, 5–7

In Psalm 84, we have one of the most beautiful and expressive of the songs of Zion (the others can be found in Psalms 46, 48, 76, 87 and 122). The lyrical beauty of the verse is highly evocative, and scholars believe it is likely that these psalms were originally sung or recited by pilgrims as they made their way towards Jerusalem for the religious festivals. Verse 1 seems to express the pilgrims' joy on catching their first glimpse of the temple, an experience that is reflected upon more deeply as the psalm progresses. Significantly, alongside the physical journey to Jerusalem, the psalmist acknowledges the existence of a parallel inner pilgrimage, when he exclaims, 'Happy are those whose strength is in you, *in whose heart are the highways to Zion*' (v. 5, my italics).

Since the dawn of time, two parallel needs have lived in tension within the human heart. First comes our need to belong—to *this* place, *this* person or family. Alongside this develops a need to explore beyond our 'safe' boundaries—to journey or to make pilgrimage. The contradiction between the two is apparent rather than real. However unconscious the desire, however blind or incoherent, the fundamental yearning to belong reaches out to God who is our true home, who calls us to journey back to the one whose creative love brought us into being.

Evidence of the perpetual existence of these two paradoxical but equal realities is woven throughout scripture. Although the term itself is not used, the concept of 'pilgrimage' as a journey taken to a sacred place because of religious conviction existed in remote antiquity. Abraham journeyed to Mount Moriah for the intended sacrifice of Isaac (Genesis 22:2). The Israelites wandered through the wilderness for 40 years on their journey to the promised land (the books of Exodus and Joshua), and Elijah made a 40-day journey through the wilderness to Horeb, the mountain of God (1 Kings 19). Until AD70, when the temple was destroyed, the Passover festival was celebrated in Jerusalem, and as many Jews as were able made the annual pilgrimage for the celebration. Indeed, the entire biblical narrative can be seen as a drama of pilgrimage and return. It is an epic journey, taking us from Genesis' allegorical account of humanity's original innocence and intimacy with God in the garden of Eden to humanity's final return to God in the new Jerusalem (Revelation 21:2–4).

Any thoughts of our possible pre-existence in God are inevitably shrouded in mystery and 'unknowing', yet there are scriptural hints. The psalmist believed that God's eyes beheld his 'unformed substance' when his body was being made 'in secret, intricately woven in the depths of the earth'

(Psalm 139:15–16). Even more startling are God's words to Jeremiah: 'Before I formed you in the womb, I knew you' (Jeremiah 1:5). This is a theme picked up more directly by the poet William Wordsworth in his poem 'Intimations of Immortality from Recollections of Early Childhood' (1807):

> But trailing clouds of glory do we come
> From God, who is our home:
> Heaven lies about us in our infancy!

The scholar and writer Ian Bradley's definition of pilgrimage holds true for all ages. He describes it 'as a departure from daily life on a journey in search of spiritual well-being. It involves leaving home, making a journey, arriving at a destination that usually has some spiritual significance, and then returning home.'[37] It is a journey that people are making in increasing numbers today.

The wanderlust of the early Irish saints has been well documented,[38] their many journeys being undertaken for a variety of reasons. For some, living on the poverty-stricken fringes of the then-known world, the reasons may have been entirely pragmatic—to escape the ravages of famine and plague at home. Others journeyed far from home in order to attend schools of spiritual instruction or for the work of mission. Yet others set out simply for the love of God, trusting their coracles to the mercy of wind and wave. For some, their pilgrimage may have been an act of penance, and it is possible that this could have been the reason for Columba's journey to Iona,[39] where the monastery he founded there became the distant ancestor of the present-day Iona community.

There had always been a spiritually heightened sense of the sacredness of the 'holy places' associated with the life of

Christ, but, as time moved on and our islands began to grow their own saints, the practice of pilgrimage to the shrine of a saint or martyr developed further. One of the most popular in England was the shrine of St Thomas à Becket at Canterbury; and the 14th-century *Canterbury Tales* by Geoffrey Chaucer brings one such pilgrimage to colourfully graphic (and sometimes riotous) life. Chaucer wickedly reminds us that not all reasons for pilgrimage are overtly 'holy': then, as now, human motives are mixed. A ninth-century Irish source was aware of this and sounded a gentle warning: 'The king you seek you'll find in Rome, it's true,/But only if he travels on the way with you.'[40]

The inner spiritual journey needs to accompany the outer physical one because, whether we think in terms of measured time or of eternity, our destination and ultimate home is in God.

For reflection and prayer

Jesus prepares to wash his disciples' feet the night before his death: 'And during supper Jesus, knowing that the Father had given all things into his hands, and that he had come from God and was going to God, got up from the table, took off his outer robe, and tied a towel around himself.'

JOHN 13:2b–4

A question

'Journeying' is a common metaphor for the spiritual life. How deeply does this metaphor speak to your own experience?

Wednesday

Place

Thus all the work that Solomon did for the house of the Lord
was finished. Solomon brought in the things that his father
David had dedicated, and stored the silver, the gold, and
all the vessels in the treasuries of the house of God. Then
Solomon assembled the elders of Israel and all the heads of
the tribes... to bring up the ark of the covenant of the Lord
out of the city of David, which is Zion... And all the elders of
Israel came, and the Levites carried the ark. So they brought
up the ark, the tent of meeting, and all the holy vessels that
were in the tent; the priests and the Levites brought them
up... Then the priests brought the ark of the covenant of the
Lord to its place, in the inner sanctuary of the house, in the
most holy place, under the wings of the cherubim... There
was nothing in the ark except the two tablets that Moses put
there at Horeb, where the Lord made a covenant with the
people of Israel after they came out of Egypt.

2 CHRONICLES 5:1–7, 10 (ABRIDGED)

Yesterday we focused on one of the Songs of Zion, which were
probably originally sung by pilgrims approaching the temple
in Jerusalem. Today we go back to the very beginnings of that
tradition, with the completion of the first temple (v. 1) and
the establishment of the holy place to house the ark of the
covenant (vv. 7, 10). This was a significant spiritual landmark:
the ark symbolised the presence of God, so it became the

focus of prayer and worship for all Israelites, whether or not they lived in Jerusalem. The link between the two themes is unmistakable: the establishment of a sacred place inevitably drew people to it, and pilgrimage became an integral part of their religious tradition.

The sacred place was also an important feature of early pagan religion, and nor was it confined within the boundaries of the Judeo-Christian tradition. All of the major world faiths have their sacred places, and it is perhaps in this fact that much of the challenge and complexity lies. The scholar Susan White writes of the destruction and bloodshed that tend to follow when the ownership of sacred sites is contested or their presence resented: 'A mosque located on a Hindu pilgrimage site in North India is demolished, and there is bloodshed, hundreds and hundreds killed... Aboriginal peoples in Australia and Canada take up arms in order to protect their ancestral sacred places, while synagogues are bombed in the former East Germany.'[41] From the First Crusade at the end of the eleventh century right up to the present day, the Holy Land has been a battleground as Jews, Christians and Muslims have fought bitterly to assert their presumed right of ownership.

In our own islands, the passing centuries brought a mush-rooming of holy sites and sacred places. One of the most famous is Iona, the tiny Scottish island that was the final landfall of Columba after his voyage from Ireland; another is Lindisfarne, the windswept tidal island just off the north-east coast of England, where Aidan planted the spiritual seed that blossomed into the Christian faith of the Northumbrian people. St Albans celebrates the first British martyr, beheaded by the Romans in AD308 for refusing to renounce his Chris-tian faith. Ireland abounds with sites of great antiquity, many of which are well-known and well-trodden features of the tourist trail. The Hill of Tara in County Meath has been a sacred site since prehistoric times but, from the fifth century AD, came to have an association with St Patrick; the remains of the monastic 'city' of Glendalough in County Wicklow stand as a testament to its seventh-century founder, the hermit-monk St Kevin. There are countless other, smaller sites, such as the holy wells of Wales that lie off the beaten track, which still carry their own aura of holiness and mystery.

With so many religious sites and artefacts, the political and the religious frequently became intertwined. The historian Janet Backhouse has written of Durham Cathedral and the Lindisfarne Gospels as 'two of the supreme masterpieces of English medieval art'.[42] Created within 75 miles of each other, they were both dedicated to St Cuthbert as well as to God's glory; but, she continues, they are 'separated by almost exactly four centuries in time, and mirror the ideals, philosophies, and spiritual needs of two very different periods in history'.[43] The Lindisfarne Gospels were created on the island by Eadfrith, Bishop of Lindisfarne, in the closing years of the seventh century. It is a glorious work and an evident labour of love. The biblical text, interwoven with intricate and often humorous artistic representations of the animal world, testifies to God's gratuitous self-giving through the glories of his creation. Durham Cathedral, however, home to the shrines of both Cuthbert and the Venerable Bede, was built side by side with the Norman castle. Apart from the site's continuing religious significance, this dramatic juxtaposition also speaks of the powerful, if at times uneasy relationship that existed between church and State in post-conquest England.

While he was Provost at Portsmouth Cathedral in the early 1980s, the retired Bishop of Salisbury David Stancliffe reordered the building, with the aim of addressing the 'all too human hierarchy' that the traditional late-medieval division between nave, chancel, choir and sanctuary suggested. The desire was to return to an earlier model, where the focus of the building plan was not hierarchy but personal and communal participation in worship. Two basic 'rooms' (for the celebration of the Word and for the receiving of the sacraments) suggest a dynamic sense of movement, with believers growing in and through worship as they are led on their journey towards God. This movement is enacted powerfully at Portsmouth in each celebration of adult baptism and confirmation, when the entire congregation accompanies the candidates round the cathedral as they journey from lectern and pulpit to baptistery, chancel and altar.

Our sacred sites have attained their standing today for a rich complexity of reasons. Whatever their pattern of development, their magnetic appeal continues, inviting us to immerse ourselves in the prayer of centuries, seeking the God who calls all people, across time and all historical circumstances, into the fullness of his love.

For reflection and prayer

Then Jacob woke from his sleep and said, 'Surely the Lord is in this place—and I did not know it! And he was afraid, and said, 'How awesome is this place! This is none other than the house of God, and this is the gate of heaven.'

GENESIS 28:16–17

A question

Think of a place that has been of particular significance to you. In what ways have your experience of that place, and your continuing memories of it, nourished your spirit?

Retreat and renew

God saw everything that he had made, and indeed, it was very good. And there was evening and there was morning, the sixth day. Thus the heavens and the earth were finished, and all their multitude. And on the seventh day God finished the work that he had done, and he rested on the seventh day from all the work that he had done. So God blessed the seventh day and hallowed it, because on it God rested from all the work that he had done in creation.

GENESIS 1:31—2:3

The Lord's my shepherd: I'll not want;
he makes me down to lie
in pastures green: he leadeth me
the quiet waters by.
W. WHITTINGHAM

The first verse of the metrical version of Psalm 23, set to the hymn tune Crimond, is one of the most well-known and well-loved of all hymns. It is one of those most frequently requested at both weddings and funerals, being popular among churchgoers and non-churchgoers alike. Universally loved the hymn may be, yet, ironically, it speaks of a divine gift that we perhaps find one of the most difficult and challenging. The words may spring easily to our lips but the invitation to set down our burdens, retreat for a while and allow the living Christ to renew, refresh and restore us is one that we often find very difficult to accept. Why should this be?

Today's passage from Genesis opens as the powerful, rhythmical first account of the creation that occupies chapter 1 draws to its close. The repetitive structure and measured rhythm of the whole account has a cumulative effect, highlighting and stressing the importance of the seventh day. This is depicted as the summit of the whole creative process, and, although these verses bring a sense of completion, the biblical text makes it quite clear that the sabbath rest that follows is to be seen as far more than an 'extra', tacked on after the real work has been accomplished. The writer gives this point a clear emphasis, stating that 'God blessed the seventh day and hallowed it, because on it God rested from all the work that he had done in creation' (2:3). The divine imperative to rest is unavoidable, and whether we interpret the 'days' of creation as literal or metaphorical is irrelevant here. Either way, the relentless rhythm of work and rest is deeply written into the very fabric of creation, and it is the whole pattern which is important. In the words of the Old Testament scholar Terence E. Fretheim, 'Creation thus has to do, not simply with spatial order, but with temporal order as well.'[44]

So why do we find this rhythm so difficult to achieve within our own lives? Intensive farming practices (where even the land is prevented from 'resting'), the development of computer technology and flexible working patterns have long broken up the age-old pattern. Thomas Edison's invention of electric light in 1878 meant that even the natural age-old patterns of sleeping and waking were no longer inviolable.

Inevitably, perhaps, the church has not been immune to the change. Continually anxious over falling numbers, the institution frequently seems to try to justify its existence through the same kind of feverish activity found in society as a whole, rather than challenging that outlook by setting out a radically different pattern.

Yet increasing numbers of people, both inside and outside the church, are looking for a different pattern, one that will bring rest and refreshment and the restoration of a healthier life/spirit balance. The enduring and increasing popularity of pilgrimage places such as Iona and Lindisfarne testify to this search, drawing visitors from across the world. In the introduction to this book, we reflected on the BBC/Worth Abbey television series *The Monastery* and the impact it had not only on the lives of the five men most immediately involved but also on the thousands of others whom the programmes touched.[45] Retreat houses throughout the country and abroad report burgeoning numbers, as increasing numbers of people begin to acknowledge the imbalance in their way of living.

So how might we reconnect with the experience of 'sabbath rest'? Despite the huge popularity of retreats, there remains a difficulty at parish level, where the pressure to be feverishly and continuously active is sometimes overwhelming. Several years ago, I spent time with a woman who was hugely committed in the work of her parish church. She came to me in great distress: because of a whole sequence of (different) church meetings in which she and her husband were respectively involved, they had hardly seen each other for the previous fortnight. They were 'ships that pass in the night', she said; church expectations were high and their marriage was coming under increasing strain.

Perhaps the first need, after we have acknowledged there is a problem, is to learn to say 'No'. This may require a courageous honesty concerning the level of our own neediness—our need to feel useful or to be liked, respected, or whatever. The other side of that coin is our fear of the nagging questions that lurk just below the level of our consciousness: if I am not *doing*, what is my purpose? If I step aside from the hurley-burley for a time and simply sit still in God's presence, what might be asked of me?

There are no easy answers, but the challenge remains. In the midst of an intensely busy ministry, Jesus regularly spent nights alone in prayer and insisted that his disciples took time for rest and refreshment after an intense period of activity (Mark 6:30–32). I think it was John Wesley who is reported to have said that he had such a busy day ahead of him that he couldn't afford to spend less than two hours in prayer. Regular periods of sabbath time dedicated to God—whether for ten minutes, several hours or days—will deepen our relationship with him, sharpen our discernment, revitalise our energies and help us to see the joys and duties of our lives within a God-given perspective.

For reflection and prayer

[Jesus said,] 'Come to me, all you that are weary and are carrying heavy burdens, and I will give you rest. Take my yoke upon you, and learn from me; for I am gentle and humble in heart, and you will find rest for your souls. For my yoke is easy, and my burden is light.'

MATTHEW 11:28–30

A question

Consider the work/rest balance in your life as it is at the moment. Do any adjustments need to be made?

Friday

Mountains and hills

On this mountain the Lord of hosts will make for all peoples a feast of rich food, a feast of well-matured wines, of rich food filled with marrow, of well-matured wines strained clear. And he will destroy on this mountain the shroud that is cast over all peoples, the sheet that is spread over all nations; he will swallow up death for ever. Then the Lord God will wipe away the tears from all faces, and the disgrace of his people he will take away from all the earth, for the Lord has spoken. It will be said on that day, Lo, this is our God; we have waited for him, so that he might save us. This is the Lord for whom we have waited; let us be glad and rejoice in his salvation. For the hand of the Lord will rest on this mountain.

ISAIAH 25:6–10

In the northern part of my native county of Lancashire, in a landscape of wild and desolate beauty, lies the prominent and distinctive landmass that is Pendle Hill.[46] Rising dramatically out of its setting as if it were England's answer to Ayers Rock, its humpbacked shape and dramatic steep slopes create an unmistakable landmark that is visible (in good weather) from 50 miles away. Although relatively modest in height at 557m, this isolated peak of the Pennine chain stands proud and clear amid the flat land surrounding it. The hill is steeped in myth and legend, most notoriously perhaps in its connection with the famous Pendle witch trials of 1612, but its significance for us concerns an altogether different spiritual association, relating to the beginnings of the Quaker movement.

George Fox (1624–91) was born in Leicestershire, the son of a prosperous Puritan weaver. As a young man, he struggled with periods of melancholy and religious doubt, which prompted him to adopt the life of an itinerant shoemaker and travel the country, seeking spiritual guidance from clergymen and others. This was not a positive experience and it led him to break away from the established church, as he became convinced that all earthly authority, whether of church or state, was corrupt. He believed that God communicated with individuals directly through the 'inner light', and, as he travelled around, he gathered small groups of followers who eventually became known as Quakers. In his journal, Fox describes a powerful religious experience that proved to be a key factor in the development of the Quaker movement:

As we travelled we came near a very great hill, called Pendle-Hill, and I was moved of the Lord to go to the top of it; which I did with difficulty, it was so very steep and high. When I was come to the top, I saw the sea bordering on Lancashire, and there, on the top, I was moved to sound the day of the Lord, and the Lord let me see in what places He had a great people to be gathered.[47]

In a sense, there was nothing new about this experience, as George Fox was following in a long and hallowed tradition of religious leaders for whom the mountain top had been a special place of divine revelation. There are numerous biblical examples; we have already spent some time with Moses and his seminal encounter with God in the burning bush on Mount Horeb (Friday, Week 1). Elijah's encounter with God, also on Horeb, in 'a sound of sheer silence' (1 Kings 19:12), was transformative at a crucial stage of his life, as was Jesus' mountain-top transfiguration for his disciples (Matthew 17:1–8).

The Irish writer and theologian Noel Dermot O'Donoghue speaks of a different kind of mountain, but one that is also imbued with deep spiritual significance. He describes it as 'neither an ideal nor a mythical mountain, nor is it exactly a holy or sacred mountain in the sense of a mountain made sacred by theophany or transfiguration'.[48] We saw earlier, in the work of Ignatius (Friday, Week 2), the powerful role of the imagination as a tool in the Christian growth; and, for O'Donoghue, this mountain is also essentially a product of the religious imagination and part of the spiritual lifeblood of his people. But its roots lie buried deeply in a place that is physically real, with nothing particular to distinguish it.

No, it is a very ordinary, very physical, very material mountain, a place of sheep and kine, of peat, and of streams that one might fish in or bathe in on a summer's day. It is an elemental mountain, of earth and air and water and fire, of sun and moon and wind and rain. What makes it special for me and for the people from which I come is that it is a place of presence and a place of presences. Only those who can perceive this in its ordinariness can encounter the mountain behind the mountain.[49]

O'Donoghue speaks from within the Irish Celtic tradition, but he is quick to acknowledge that the Celts do not have a monopoly of this kind of experience: for the primal religious traditions of Australia and America, the mountain, and indeed all nature, is vibrantly alive. We see the same spiritual reality reflected also in the wider Christian tradition—for example, in the teaching of Francis of Assisi (twelfth century), the writings of the 17th-century priest-poet Thomas Traherne and, more recently, the poetry of Gerard Manley Hopkins (19th century) and R.S. Thomas (20th century).

But we conclude today where we began—with a prophecy of Isaiah and another mountain of the religious imagination. To an Israelite readership, this prophecy would have had powerful resonances, as the banquet on the mountain (v. 6) would have recalled the meal enjoyed by Moses and the elders of Israel in affirmation of the covenant on Mount Sinai (Exodus 24:9–11). It is only a brief reference, but the association with the covenant seems to give it its significance. Isaiah's mountain may well offer a powerful and spiritually emotive link with the past but its underlying purpose is eschatological. It propels us forward, in hope and great joy, to a time when God 'will destroy on this mountain the shroud that is cast over all peoples' (v. 7) and will invite them to share in his banquet in reconciliation and peace. 'Then the Lord God will wipe away the tears from all faces... For the hand of the Lord will rest on this mountain' (vv. 8 and 10).

For reflection and prayer

I lift up my eyes to the hills—from where will my help come? My help comes from the Lord, who made heaven and earth.

PSALM 121:1–2

A question

Isaiah uses the mountain as a symbol of the unity that will exist between all parts of the creation in God's kingdom. Are there ways in which we can be working towards that unity now?

Saturday

The inner cell

For God alone my soul waits in silence; from him comes my salvation. He alone is my rock and my salvation, my fortress; I shall never be shaken. How long will you assail a person, will you batter your victim, all of you, as you would a leaning wall, a tottering fence?...For God alone my soul waits in silence, for my hope is from him. He alone is my rock and my salvation, my fortress; I shall not be shaken.

PSALM 62:1–3, 5–6

'And whenever you pray, do not be like the hypocrites; for they love to stand and pray in the synagogues and at the street corners, so that they may be seen by others. Truly I tell you, they have received their reward. But whenever you pray, go into your room and shut the door and pray to your Father who is in secret; and your Father who sees in secret will reward you.

MATTHEW 6:5–6

The Irish poet and playwright W.B. Yeats was one of the most important figures in 20th-century poetry, and in 1923 he was awarded the Nobel Prize for Literature. One of his most lyrical poems is 'The Lake Isle of Innisfree' (1892), which represented, for Yeats, an enchanted place both in reality and in the imagination. Inspired by the wilderness-living experience of the American author and poet Henry David Thoreau,[50] Yeats planned to live on the little island of

Innisfree in Lough Gill. As the poem describes, he wanted to build a small cabin there 'of clay and wattles made' and to live peacefully 'alone in the bee-loud glade'. But in the final verse of the poem, Yeats touches a deeper reality. Innisfree is a very real place but verse three reveals that its power for the poet also lay in its capacity to evoke an imaginative, spiritual dimension:

> *While I stand on the roadway, or on the pavements grey,*
> *I hear it in the deep heart's core.*

It is in that reference to 'the deep heart's core' that Yeats touches on our focus for today's reflection—the inner cell of the heart. During Week 2 we considered several different aspects of prayer, and today we take it a stage further. We use two biblical texts to help us in this, one from each Testament. The verses from Matthew's Gospel come from an extended section containing much of Jesus' teaching on prayer (ch. 6), and here Jesus is helping his disciples to distinguish true prayer from that which is a sham. Genuine prayer, says Jesus, occurs within the intimate context of the Father–child relationship and springs from humility and a deep awareness of personal sin. The instruction to 'go into your room and shut the door' (v. 6) can refer equally to the outward action and to the process that takes place secretly in the 'inner cell' of the heart.

Written many centuries earlier, the words of the psalmist also seem to be pointing towards this reality. He feels himself to be besieged on every side, with words such as 'assail' and 'batter' reinforcing the sense of being under attack. By contrast, God is experienced as a 'rock' and a 'fortress' in whom he finds security: 'I shall never be shaken' (v. 2). The

A question

Many Christians speak of the strength they receive from being present with Christ in their 'inner cell', even in the midst of activity. Is this a reality in your experience? If not, are there ways in which you could nurture it?

Week 4

Week 4

Me and my shadow

Hidden in the shadow

For we know that the law is spiritual; but I am of the flesh, sold into slavery under sin. I do not understand my own actions. For I do not do what I want, but I do the very thing I hate. Now if I do what I do not want, I agree that the law is good. But in fact it is no longer I that do it, but sin that dwells within me. For I know that nothing good dwells in me, that is, in my flesh. I can will what is right, but I cannot do it. For I do not do the good I want, but the evil I do not want is what I do.

ROMANS 7:14–19

The passage above offers us a tiny glimpse into Paul's thought on the human experience of trying to live a spiritual life. These few short verses are a small part of his extensive argument (Romans 7:1—8:11) on the role and significance of the law (the Torah) in the life of believers. In a somewhat convoluted passage, Paul seems nevertheless to put his finger on one of the main problems of the human condition—that however good our intentions may be, we are experts, because of sin, at sabotaging our own efforts to live a good and spiritual life. 'For I do not do the good I want, but the evil I do not want is what I do' (v. 19). Scholars have explored Paul's arguments on sin and the law elsewhere, fruitfully and in depth,[56] but we focus today on a slightly different perspective.

What Paul managed to identify was the fact that, when it

comes to understanding the motivation for the way we think or behave, we have only limited awareness. Sometimes our reasoning may appear to us to be absolutely clear; we think we know exactly what we are doing and why. At other times the reasons for our behaviour may not be anything like as clear, and on such occasions we may make statements such as 'I don't know what came over me!' or 'Whatever got into me?' We become uncomfortably aware that our feelings, attitudes and ways of being in the world are frequently unpredictable. We all like to feel we are in control, so the realisation that the shape of our personalities and the root causes of our behaviour are largely hidden from us is not a comfortable one.

The psychological concept of the unconscious is a relatively recent one, but Paul was clearly aware of its effects. During the early years of the 20th century, two European psychiatrists, Sigmund Freud and Carl Gustav Jung, rose to prominence. Originally they were friends and allies, united in their work on the unconscious, but their paths diverged acrimoniously when they found themselves in sharp disagreement over their respective interpretations of dream symbolism. During the rest of this week we shall be exploring different aspects of a phenomenon that was a key element of Jung's philosophy of the unconscious—the shadow.

In the physical world around us, the significance of the shadow lies in the fact that it gives objects shape, form and substance. Without it, we would inhabit a flat and two-dimensional world, a little like the scenes in the paintings of L.S. Lowry. Jung was the first to see a parallel to the shadow within the human personality. For him, the shadow is buried deep in our unconscious and contains repressed fears, weaknesses, instincts and shortcomings, including aspects of personality that society deems to be unacceptable. Freud's theory had a similar element, which he named the id, but he viewed its contents very differently. For Freud, the id was the container of all that was primitive and dangerous in the human personality, while Jung's interpretation of the same concept was far more positive. We may be fearful of what we cannot fully see or understand, but Jung came to believe that the shadow was, nevertheless, a place of hidden treasure. Consequently, the careful integration of the hidden contents of the shadow into the person's conscious life was vital, because anything that remained ignored and unintegrated had the capacity to warp a person's energies and potentialities, becoming harmful and destructive. Faith and spirituality—or their lack—were seen as playing an essential part in this process. While not claiming an adherence to any faith in particular, Jung believed that a person could never be fully whole without the integration of the spiritual dimension of experience into that person's conscious life.[57]

We may feel apprehensive or unsure about this process and uncertain about what we might be letting ourselves in for. If that is the case, God's words to King Cyrus through the prophet Isaiah (which we shall explore in some detail on Friday) may offer us encouragement: 'I will give you the treasures of darkness and riches hidden in secret places, so that you may know that it is I, the Lord, the God of Israel, who call you by your name' (Isaiah 45:3).

For the rest of this week, with the help of scripture, we shall be exploring the shadow in some of its different aspects.

For reflection and prayer

You desire truth in the inward being; therefore teach me wisdom in my secret heart.

PSALM 51:6

'There is nothing hidden, except to be disclosed; nor is anything secret, except to come to light.'

MARK 4:22

A question

What do you think of Jung's concept of the 'shadow'? Does it resonate with any of your own life experience?

Monday

The elder son

'Now his elder son was in the field; and when he came and approached the house, he heard music and dancing. He called one of the slaves and asked what was going on. He replied, "Your brother has come, and your father has killed the fatted calf, because he has got him back safe and sound." Then he became angry and refused to go in. His father came out and began to plead with him. But he answered his father, "Listen! For all these years I have been working like a slave for you, and I have never disobeyed your command; yet you have never given me even a young goat so that I might celebrate with my friends. But when this son of yours came back, who has devoured your property with prostitutes, you killed the fatted calf for him!" Then the father said to him, "Son, you are always with me, and all that is mine is yours. But we had to celebrate and rejoice, because this brother of yours was dead and has come to life; he was lost and has been found."'

LUKE 15:25–32

We have travelled some way on our Lenten journey, but today we revisit briefly the point of our departure. On Ash Wednesday we reflected on the parable of the prodigal son, focussing specifically on the behaviour of the younger son and his relationship with his father.

If we are serious about our desire to welcome the way of

the cross in our lives, we will find that one of the inevitable consequences is the need to face up to, and accept, our human sin and frailty. This week, we will be focusing on the role of the 'shadow' in our lives, and we will be using incidents from scripture to help us reflect on this more hidden (and often more feared) side of our humanity. The richness of the parables lies partly in their uncompromising truthfulness and the way they invite us, if we will, to identify with their characters and see them as a mirror to our own human nature. As a parent, we may find it all too easy to step into the shoes of the father, loving and waiting and longing for the return of a wayward son or daughter. As a young person, we may readily feel for the younger son, restless and impatient with the traditional ways of his father and eager to make his own way in the world. A more responsible child may have no difficulty in feeling for the elder son. Today, as we seek to walk in the way of the cross, we are invited to gaze steadfastly into the mirror held up to us by the attitude and behaviour of the eldest son in this parable.

There is much here that may cause us to rise up in sympathy and solidarity with him. We have heard nothing of his story until this point, other than the very brief statement in verse 11: 'There was a man who had two sons.' We don't know how this son felt about his younger brother's desertion: was he angry, resentful, envious that his sibling had been allowed his bid for freedom while he himself remained trapped by his work on his father's land? For most of the parable, the focus remains on the younger son, so we don't know any of this directly, but, with his masterly storyteller's art, Jesus tells us much in the concluding short conversation between the father and his elder boy: 'Listen! For all these years I have been working like a slave for you, and I have never disobeyed your command; yet you have never given me even a young goat so that I might celebrate with my friends' (v. 29).

We can perhaps imagine a young man who is a dutiful son, quieter and less brash than his younger brother, faithfully bearing the burden of the heavy farm work and without complaint. But the triumphant return of his brother and the celebrations that accompany it prove too much, and the anger and resentment that have been burning like a slow fuse for so many years finally explode into passionate life. In his anger, he disowns his brother: note the sneering reference to 'this son of yours... who has devoured your property' (v. 30). We may well experience some empathy with his feelings, but we marvel at his father's response: anger is not matched with anger, but the elder son receives the same compassion and healing love as his younger brother. The elder son, in his hurt and resentment, disowns his relationship to his brother ('this son of yours'), but immediately the father lovingly and firmly restores it ('this brother of yours', v. 32). Along with the gentle insistence on the restoration of family bonds, there is also fairness. All is not to be exactly as it was before, because the father reassures his eldest son that 'you are always with me, and all that is mine is yours' (v. 31). It is right that the returning prodigal should be joyfully welcomed back into the family circle, but the father's remaining inheritance belongs to the elder son.

It is not comfortable to be faced so uncompromisingly with the reality of aspects of the 'shadow' side of our human nature. When Shakespeare's Hamlet directs the company of actors who have come to perform at the royal court, he instructs them to act so as to hold 'the mirror up to nature' (Act III, Scene 2), and much of scripture does precisely this for us. We may like to think of ourselves as loving, charitable, caring and tolerant people, but if we ask God to reveal the truth to us, parables such as this one quickly reveal our tendency to descend into envy, spite and pettiness whenever our self-interest is challenged. But God's standards of fairness and justice refuse to be confined by our human limitations, and he constantly works with us, if we will let him, to heal relationships and restore us to the all-embracing circle of his love.

For reflection and prayer

Peter turned and saw the disciple whom Jesus loved following them... When Peter saw him, he said to Jesus, 'Lord, what about him?' Jesus said to him, 'If it is my will that he remain until I come, what is that to you? Follow me!'

JOHN 21:20–22 (ABRIDGED)

A question

When you are asked to undertake a piece of work, how easy is it simply to focus on the task in hand without comparing it with what has (or hasn't) been asked of others?

Tuesday

Jekyll and Hyde

Now when Jesus came into the district of Caesarea Philippi, he asked his disciples, 'Who do people say that the Son of Man is?' And they said, 'Some say John the Baptist, but others Elijah, and still others Jeremiah or one of the prophets.' He said to them, 'But who do you say that I am?' Simon Peter answered, 'You are the Messiah, the Son of the living God.' And Jesus answered him, 'Blessed are you, Simon son of Jonah! For flesh and blood has not revealed this to you, but my Father in heaven. And I tell you, you are Peter, and on this rock I will build my church, and the gates of Hades will not prevail against it...'

From that time on, Jesus began to show his disciples that he must go to Jerusalem and undergo great suffering at the hands of the elders and chief priests and scribes, and be killed, and on the third day be raised. And Peter took him aside and began to rebuke him, saying, 'God forbid it, Lord! This must never happen to you.' But he turned and said to Peter, 'Get behind me, Satan! You are a stumbling-block to me; for you are setting your mind not on divine things but on human things.'

MATTHEW 16:13–18, 21–23

Peter's confession of faith in Jesus as Messiah at Caesarea Philippi is presented as one of the principal Christological cornerstones of the Gospel. It is a confession that Jesus

138

consciously seeks to elicit, coming as the climax to his questioning of the disciples as to who people think that he is. The disciples' responses are wide-ranging and various ('Some say... but others... and still others...' v. 14), but Jesus is not content with vague generalisations and pushes them for their own thoughts (v. 15, 'But who do you say that I am?'). In keeping with what we know of his character, it is Peter who immediately speaks up (v. 16, 'You are the Messiah').

Peter is not alone in the Gospels in this flash of inspiration. In John's Gospel, John the Baptist acknowledges Jesus' true identity to two of his disciples (John 1:36), and the Samaritan villagers, introduced to Jesus by the woman he met at the well, declare their awareness of his divinity on their own account (John 4:42, 'It is no longer because of what you said that we believe, for we have heard for ourselves, and we know that this is truly the Saviour of the world'). Slightly disturbingly, perhaps, such insightful glimpses are also put into the mouths of demons and unclean spirits (Mark 1:24, 'I know who you are, the Holy One of God'; Luke 4:41, 'You are the Son of God!').

So what is so special about this particular incident? It is not as if the disciples have had no glimpse of Jesus' identity up to this point. After Jesus had saved Peter from drowning in the windswept waters of the Sea of Galilee, the disciples had worshipped Jesus as the Son of God (Matthew 14:33). But this incident at Caesarea Philippi is the first time that Jesus has directly pushed the disciples for a response, and Peter is instantly rewarded with praise and a rich blessing.

Hidden in the language used is a clue to the truth of what has happened here. Jesus' praise of Peter is not the equivalent of a teacher praising a schoolboy who has come up with a particularly clever answer. The 'right answer' has nothing at all to do with Peter's cleverness and everything to do with the action of God. The Greek word for 'reveal' or 'unveil', *apocalyptō*, refers to the divine disclosure of an apocalyptic secret, not a personal, individual spiritual experience. In the words of the New Testament scholar M. Eugene Boring, 'Peter is not blessed because of a personal attainment or insight he has achieved. Knowledge of Jesus' saving role comes by divine revelation—as gift, not attainment.'[58]

If Peter was tempted to rest on his spiritual laurels, so to speak, it wasn't long before he found himself being brought down to earth with a bump. From the high point of 'You are the Messiah, the Son of the living God' (Matthew 16:16), Jesus then begins to unfold for his disciples just what his messiahship is going to entail. On hearing that it will involve great suffering and, ultimately, death, Peter again jumps in impulsively: 'God forbid it, Lord! This must never happen to you!' (v. 22).

We can see Peter's response in two ways and probably resonate to some extent with both. First there is the personal gut-reaction that we inevitably experience when someone we love is under threat or in some kind of danger; if there was anything we could do to avert the danger, we would. Second, we may also be able to understand Peter's difficulty in grasping the true nature of Jesus' messiahship—a difficulty he shared with most of the people of his time. Eugene Boring comments, 'Despite his revelation from God (16:17), Peter continues to think as good human beings are accustomed to think: reasonably, egocentrically, and in terms of human friendship and "success".'[59]

The fact that Peter is capable of divine insight and then, almost immediately, is able to get things completely wrong should be a great encouragement to us. The nature of Jesus' identity and the meaning of discipleship are truths that are learned gradually along the way, rather than instantly, once and for all. There is comfort here for all of us who may be concerned about past mistakes and misunderstandings, and with the guarantee of more to come in the future. But there is a warning too for those times when we think we do understand and, as a result, close our minds and hearts to any possibility of further growth.

For reflection and prayer

Do not be conformed to this world, but be transformed by the renewing of your minds, so that you may discern what is the will of God—what is good and acceptable and perfect.

ROMANS 12:2

A question

Who do *you* think that Jesus is? Does the conclusion you come to make any difference to the way you live your life?

Wednesday

The shadow and dreaming

Jacob left Beer-sheba and went towards Haran. He came to a certain place and stayed there for the night, because the sun had set. Taking one of the stones of the place, he put it under his head and lay down in that place. And he dreamed that there was a ladder set up on the earth, the top of it reaching to heaven; and the angels of God were ascending and descending on it. And the Lord stood beside him and said, 'I am the Lord, the God of Abraham your father and the God of Isaac; the land on which you lie I will give to you and to your offspring; and your offspring shall be like the dust of the earth, and you shall spread abroad to the west and to the east and to the north and to the south; and all the families of the earth shall be blessed in you and in your offspring. Know that I am with you and will keep you wherever you go, and will bring you back to this land; for I will not leave you until I have done what I promised you.' Then Jacob woke from his sleep and said, 'Surely the Lord is in this place—and I did not know it!' And he was afraid, and said, 'How awesome is this place! This is none other than the house of God, and this is the gate of heaven.'

GENESIS 28:10–17

Many years ago, my husband and I were planning to move house. We had been looking for some time at possible properties in our local area when we came across a beautiful cottage on the outskirts of a village. The setting was idyllic: the cottage was set back from the lane up a grassy slope, and it looked out on to the fields and woods of an unspoilt country estate. What's more—and even more miraculous— it was actually within our price range. I wanted to put in an offer on the spot, and remember being somewhat reluctant when my husband wisely advised that we 'sleep on it' before coming to any decision.

That night, I found myself back at the cottage in my dreams. The setting was just as we had seen it—but what a difference in my feelings about it all! My dreaming self was not seduced by the quaintness of the cottage and the beauty of the surroundings, as my waking self had been, but rather saw the reality that my conscious mind had been determined not to see. The cottage was really rather small and cramped; even the largest bedroom wasn't big enough for our five-foot bed *and* two bedside tables, and there was virtually no storage space. Living there would only be possible for us, I realised, if we were able to get permission to build large extensions at the back and out over the garage—permission we were by no means certain to be granted in a conservation area. I awoke with the dream's sense of realism deeply impressed on my mind, and was thankful that my husband's restraint the previous day had saved us from what could have been quite a costly mistake.

One of the fundamental tenets of the Christian faith lies in the belief that we are in relationship with a God who loves us passionately, endlessly and utterly beyond our deserving. Both the Old and New Testaments reveal the fact that God communicates this love to us in a variety of ways—through prophecy and the written word, through human relationships and the beauties of creation, and through dreams. In today's passage we focus on a particularly rich example—the dream of Jacob, which was to prove to be a hugely significant turning point in his life.

Up to this point, Jacob's track record was not one to be particularly proud of. He had recently cheated his twin brother Esau out of both his birthright as the eldest twin (Genesis 25:29–34), and his father Isaac's blessing (Genesis 27). At the time when his dream occurred, Jacob was on his way to the house of his uncle Laban, with a view to choosing a wife from among his uncle's daughters.

The religious significance of this particular biblical dream was relevant not only for Jacob but for the whole future nation of Israel. Up to this moment, God's relationship with humanity had been distinctly one-sided: he was perceived as relating to individuals, directly or through intermediaries, but the individual concerned had no automatic right of reply. With this dream, there is a seismic shift: angels ascend and descend the ladder set up between heaven and earth, indicating that from this point on, 'the traffic of the Spirit which had been so uncompromisingly from above to below, now was suddenly transformed into a two-way affair also possible from below to above'.[60] Jacob's environment becomes transfigured and, with a sudden flash of insight, he sees that the God who is directing his life is a personal God.

The encouragement to 'sleep on' a knotty problem embodies an age-old wisdom, capable of interpretation on both the spiritual and psychological levels. Perhaps, in the end, it really doesn't matter whether we interpret the message of our dream psychologically, spiritually or both. In either case, the endlessly swirling currents that make up the constant busyness of our conscious mind come temporarily to rest, allowing truths and realities hidden in the unconscious to rise to the surface, releasing previously unknown possibilities. Until now we may or may not have given our dreamlife much attention, but much of the biblical material on dreams challenges us to take them seriously. If we are able to approach our dreams prayerfully, asking God to use them as one of the channels of his communication to us, then we, like Jacob, may find our experience transfigured, enabling us to continue our journey with a new and deeper sense of God's purposes in our lives and our place within them.

For reflection and prayer

'In the last days it will be, God declares, that I will pour out my Spirit upon all flesh, and your sons and daughters shall prophesy, and your young men shall see visions, and your old men shall dream dreams.'

ACTS 2:17; QUOTING JOEL 2:28

A question

In what ways might our dreams help us to discern the purposes of God in our lives more fruitfully?

Thursday

Wrestling with God

The same night he got up and took his two wives, his two maids, and his eleven children, and crossed the ford of the Jabbok. He took them and sent them across the stream, and likewise everything that he had. Jacob was left alone; and a man wrestled with him until daybreak. When the man saw that he did not prevail against Jacob, he struck him on the hip socket; and Jacob's hip was put out of joint as he wrestled with him. Then he said, 'Let me go, for the day is breaking.' But Jacob said, 'I will not let you go, unless you bless me.' So he said to him, 'What is your name?' And he said, 'Jacob.' Then the man said, 'You shall no longer be called Jacob, but Israel, for you have striven with God and with humans, and have prevailed.' Then Jacob asked him, 'Please tell me your name.' But he said to him, 'Why is it that you ask my name?' And there he blessed him. So Jacob called the place Peniel, saying, 'For I have seen God face to face, and yet my life is preserved.' The sun rose upon him as he passed Penuel, limping because of his hip.

GENESIS 32:22–31

The event described in this intriguing passage has significant parallels with yesterday's reading and reflection, which focused on Jacob's dream of the ladder linking heaven and earth. Both incidents are connected with Jacob's troubled relationship with his twin brother Esau. In yesterday's reading, God met Jacob through the medium of his dream at a time when he had fled the promised land in fear of his brother's righteous anger; today's meeting occurs as Jacob re-enters the promised land, again fearful of his brother's retribution. By the time he reaches the ford at Jabbok, he is attempting to move on from his dubious past. Just prior to this incident, Jacob has heard that his brother is coming to meet him (32:6), so he sends ahead several droves of animals as propitiatory gifts, in the hope of appeasing Esau's wrath (vv. 13–21). Having then sent his household across the ford, Jacob faces the mysterious stranger who appears at his side alone.

This seemingly anonymous stranger does have an identity. He names himself, and Jacob also names him, as *elohim,* one of the Hebrew names for God (vv. 28, 30). So what is going on here? The meaning of the tale is tantalisingly elusive and is consequently open to a number of different interpretations. Psychologically, some see in this event an encounter between Jacob and his shadow. Jung believed that the shadow could emerge in dreams and take various forms, animal or human. The problem with following this line of interpretation here is that Jacob's encounter with the stranger is depicted as physical, not as a dream or vision. Spiritually, it has been suggested that the encounter and its after-effects serve as God's retribution and punishment for Jacob's history of deception and double-dealing. The fact that the incident ends with God's blessing of Jacob is taken by some as indicating some kind of conversion experience on Jacob's part, but the difficulty here is that the text simply does not support it. God does not appear to condemn Jacob's previous behaviour, reprehensible as it has been; Jacob does not seem to be repentant of anything, and the later biblical narrative will demonstrate that there was to be no fundamental change in his subsequent life pattern.

The implications of this for us are both uncomfortable and strangely reassuring. The narrative appears to emphasise the mysterious fact that God will act in the lives of those whom he calls, however undeserving those lives may appear to be in human terms. The dislocation of Jacob's hip is certainly a puzzling feature, but I find myself reminded of Paul's 'thorn in the flesh' (see 2 Corinthians 12:7). It may be that, in some way that defies our human understanding, Jacob's injury, far from hindering him, actually enabled him to grow and move on in his journey. There are times when we simply have to take on trust the fact that the activity and involvement of God will take the form of 'tough love', and that it will be a far from comfortable experience at the time. The 16th-century Spanish saint Teresa of Avila is reputed to have shaken her fist at heaven on one occasion and said, 'Lord, if this is how you treat your friends, then it is no wonder you have so few of them!'

Here is another mystery: given that the Israelites did not believe that it was possible to look on the face of God and live, how did Jacob manage to survive the night's wrestling match? Surely the main reason must be that God did not appear to Jacob in all his glory here, but as a man, on Jacob's own level. It is also clear that God was not playing a child's game with Jacob. Their encounter was a genuine struggle: Jacob was neither overwhelmed nor 'allowed' to win. So it is with each one of us. Our shadow also contains feelings, longings and desires that may not have touched our conscious minds, but we can be reassured that, as he did with Jacob, God meets us just as we are, tempering his strength to ours, with an approach exactly tailored to meet the needs of which we may or may not be aware.

Like Jacob, also, we learn that our own human strength can only take us so far, and that, as we journey on, we need the support and blessing that only God can give. The theologian Terence Fretheim sees such encounters as 'divinely initiated exercises in human becoming... God's engagements in such moments in people's lives is always a gracious move, informed most basically by faithfulness to promises made, and in the interests of health, peace, and well-being.'[61]

For reflection and prayer

My child, if you accept my words and treasure up my commandments within you, making your ear attentive to wisdom and inclining your heart to understanding; if you indeed cry out for insight, and raise your voice for understanding; if you seek it like silver, and search for it as for hidden treasures—then you will understand the fear of the Lord and find the knowledge of God.

PROVERBS 2:1–5

A question

How deeply have you allowed your relationship with God to penetrate your life? Do you have a 'dislocated hip'?

Friday

Hidden riches

I will give you the treasures of darkness and riches hidden in
secret places, so that you may know that it is I, the Lord, the
God of Israel, who call you by your name.

ISAIAH 45:3

I can remember a morning a number of years ago which,
while not perhaps changing the course of my life, influenced
massively the future direction of my thinking. It was a
morning like many others: I was eating breakfast and feeding
the dog, and was generally engaged with the normal early
morning routine as I prepared to go out to work. I had the
radio on in the background as a sort of auditory wallpaper; I
wasn't really listening but at one point I became aware that
'Thought for the Day' had just begun. Then I stopped in my
tracks, listening intently.

The speaker that morning was reflecting on a verse from
Isaiah of which I had not been consciously aware before. It
was the verse quoted above: 'I will give you the treasures
of darkness and riches hidden in secret places…'. What
stunned me so completely was that I had never encountered
the idea of darkness in the Bible, viewed positively: to my
knowledge, darkness was usually employed symbolically to
represent phenomena such as chaos (Genesis 1:2), blindness
(Deuteronomy 28:29), sickness (Luke 11:34), ignorance and
confusion (Psalm 82:5), and the hiding place of evil (John

13:30), among many other negative characteristics.

This verse from Isaiah was a revelation. With growing excitement, I went searching scripture for other similar references. Was it a 'one-off' or was it part of a more positive strand of biblical tradition that had somehow gone 'underground'? My search revealed considerable evidence that the latter was the case, and a good concordance quickly revealed some exciting and challenging examples. Most startling was the idea of darkness as the dwelling place of God. This was expressed most clearly, perhaps, on the occasion when Moses, on receiving the Ten Commandments, went up Mount Sinai and 'drew near to the thick darkness where God was' (Exodus 20:21)—an idea repeated in Psalm 18:11.

The concept has other positive associations, where it relies on the idea of darkness by implication rather than by direct terminology. On Wednesday this week we considered some of the positive potentialities hidden in the 'darkness' of our unconscious dream-lives, and many of Jesus' parables rely on the imagery of new life being nurtured in the mysterious darkness of the soil (Mark 4:26–32; John 12:24–25). Even the negative association of chaos and darkness in Genesis 1 can be turned on its head: the cosmic soup that was initially a 'formless void' (Genesis 1:2) proved to be the source and seedbed of fecund and myriad forms of life.

But what about those times when the 'treasures' of darkness do not, at first sight, seem to be treasures at all? Today's short reading itself embraces two levels of hidden blessing. The first level relates to the Persian King Cyrus I, who is the subject of the prophecy of Isaiah from which this verse is taken. This king—a non-Israelite and therefore not one of the 'chosen people'—is named by Isaiah as the Lord's 'anointed' (45:1), chosen by God to be his instrument in freeing the

Israelites from exile and allowing them to return to their homeland. The experience of exile had forced the Israelites into a re-evaluation of their ideas of God and his relationship to them; here, they learn in a deeper way that God's help can come through the most unlikely of channels. The second level of hidden blessing comes in Isaiah's addressing of the prophecy as if to Cyrus himself. This foreign king, who does not know the Israelites' God, is unaware of his role in God's purposes, yet God calls him and 'surnames' him—in effect, adopts Cyrus as his son—'for the sake of my servant Jacob, and Israel my chosen' (v. 4). God does indeed move in mysterious ways.

How do we respond to God through the peaks and troughs, the intricate patterning, of our own lives? Do we recognise that God may work out his will in our lives through unexpected people and situations? Paul assures us 'that all things work together for good for those who love God, who are called according to his purpose' (Romans 8:28). This is one of the most well-known and oft-quoted verses from scripture, but how well attuned are we to the belief and trust it expresses? *All* things work together for good...? It's easy enough, perhaps, when things are going well for us; easy enough at such times for us to affirm Robert Browning's words, 'God's in his heaven—all's right with the world!' ('Pippa's song', 1841). But how do we seek for and find such trust when confronted with the shadow side of life, the tragedies that seem to have no positive answer— the massacre of children in a civil war; the death of a young mother from cancer, leaving a grieving husband and newborn baby? The examples could be multiplied endlessly and swirl around us on a daily basis. Then there are the normal areas of suffering to which none of us are immune, associated with the universal human experience of living, growing, ageing and dying. How do we respond when such 'shadow' experiences become part of the conscious, lived reality of our own lives?

When Job finally emerged from the darkness of his prolonged suffering, there were still no easy answers. What he did receive was an overwhelming affirmation of the wonder and grandeur of God's creative power, and with this came (with some sense of relief, it would seem) a humble recognition of the inadequacy of his own understanding: 'I know that you can do all things, and that no purpose of yours can be thwarted... I have uttered what I did not understand, things too wonderful for me, which I did not know' (Job 42:2–3).

For reflection and prayer

Have you not known? Have you not heard? The Lord is the everlasting God, the Creator of the ends of the earth. He does not faint or grow weary; his understanding is unsearchable. He gives power to the faint, and strengthens the powerless. Even youths will faint and be weary, and the young will fall exhausted; but those who wait for the Lord shall renew their strength, they shall mount up with wings like eagles, they shall run and not be weary, they shall walk and not faint.

ISAIAH 40:28–31

A question

Do you find the concept of darkness in relation to the spiritual life disturbing or exciting? Why?

Saturday

The soul's healer

So [Jesus] told them this parable: 'Which one of you, having a hundred sheep and losing one of them, does not leave the ninety-nine in the wilderness and go after the one that is lost until he finds it? When he has found it, he lays it on his shoulders and rejoices. And when he comes home, he calls together his friends and neighbours, saying to them, "Rejoice with me, for I have found my sheep that was lost." Just so, I tell you, there will be more joy in heaven over one sinner who repents than over ninety-nine righteous people who need no repentance.'

LUKE 15:3–7

The Lord's my shepherd: I'll not want;
he makes me down to lie
in pastures green: he leadeth me
the quiet waters by.

My soul he doth restore again,
and me to walk doth make
within the paths of righteousness
e'en for his own name's sake.
W. WHITTINGHAM

We first considered verse 1 of the well-loved hymn 'The Lord's my shepherd' on Thursday of Week 3, when we were reflecting on the value and necessity of building times of rest and retreat into our busy timetables. Today we move on to verse 2 of that hymn as we focus on the experience of Jesus as soul-healer, set within the context of the image of the good shepherd.

I have an icon of Jesus the good shepherd in my study at home, which speaks to me in a way I find both powerful and moving but difficult to put into words. It is a contemporary icon, written a few years ago (all icons are 'written' rather than painted) by a member of a small Orthodox monastic community in America.[62] The figure of Christ dominates the image and is in close focus. He is richly robed in flowing garments in graduated shades of deep red and green and carries a shepherd's staff within the crook of his left arm. Around his shoulders lies a pure white, curly-fleeced lamb, which has its eyes open and is calm and at rest. Christ's hands are holding the lamb's feet and bear the wounds of his crucifixion, and the wood of the cross is clearly visible above his halo-surrounded head and behind his shoulders. Christ's face is compelling and has been written with the enigmatic quality detectable in icons from across the centuries. There is a slight suggestion of a frown in the puckering of the skin between the eyes, but there is also an impression of great gentleness. Is Christ smiling—or not? It's hard to tell, but it doesn't really matter. It is his eyes that attract, their magnetic quality drawing the viewer in; and, with his calm but searching gaze, it is as if he is looking into the very depths of your soul.

The image of the shepherd in scripture is a prominent one and reflects the reality of a Palestinian life-setting. In the Old Testament, God is frequently described as Israel's shepherd, particularly in the Psalms (for example, 23:1–4; 28:9; 78:52;

80:1; 100:3) and the later prophets (Jeremiah 31:10; Ezekiel 34:11–22; Zechariah 13:7). In both Testaments the shepherd is used as an image for Israel's leaders, not all of whom were good and reliable (Jeremiah 3:15; John 10:1, 12–13; 1 Peter 5:2), so Jesus is at pains to claim himself to be the Good Shepherd—the one who gives his life for the sheep (John 10:11).

Today's passage is one of a trio of parables of the 'lost', alongside those of the lost coin (Luke 15:8–10) and the prodigal son (vv. 11–32). The pressure on Jesus was increasing: tax collectors and sinners were coming to listen to him, and the scribes and Pharisees were becoming increasingly unhappy about the time Jesus spent with these people (vv. 1–2). The three parables formed Jesus' response to their disquiet, making clear to the hostile authorities just how great was the value that God placed on these 'lost' ones (vv. 7, 9–10, 31–32). As Jesus made clear elsewhere, the divine response to the penitent sinner was never intended to be punishment, but rather healing and restoration (Mark 2:17).

The church has struggled to maintain this emphasis ever since, with varying degrees of success. The sixth-century Irish *Penitentials* were documents written for pastoral use in dealing with the particular sins of penitent Christians.[63] As can be seen from the Penitential of Cummean, the aim was healing rather than punishment: 'Here begins the prologue on the medicine for the salvation of souls. As we are about to speak of the remedies for wounds according to the rulings of the fathers before us… let us first indicate in a concise manner the medicines of Holy Scripture.'[64]

The same theme continues six centuries later with Aelred, the twelfth-century abbot of Rievaulx. Aelred saw his abbacy

156

in terms of shepherding and, in his 'Pastoral Prayer', he confesses to Christ his sense of utter inadequacy for the task:

> To you, I say, Good Shepherd,
> this shepherd, who is not good, makes his prayer.
> He cries to you,
> troubled upon his own account, and troubled for your sheep.[65]

After earnestly seeking Christ's help for the work to which he has been called, he concludes with a passionate plea for healing:

> Lord, look at my soul's wounds.
> Your living and effective eye sees everything.
> It pierces like a sword, even to part asunder soul and
> spirit.
>
> And as I thus resist,
> do you the while heal all my weakness perfectly,
> cure all my wounds, and put back into shape
> all my deformities.
> Lord, may your good, sweet Spirit
> descend into my heart,
> and fashion there a dwelling for himself...
> disposing it to penitence and love and gentleness.[66]

For reflection and prayer

O Lord my God, I cried to you for help, and you have healed me... You have turned my mourning into dancing; you have taken off my sackcloth and clothed me with joy, so that my soul may praise you and not be silent. O Lord my God, I will give thanks to you for ever.

PSALM 30:2, 11–12

A question

In the Irish tradition, penance was looked on not as punishment but as 'medicine for the soul'. How does this approach compare with your own experience?

Week 5

Open to the world

Beyond the house of Israel

Now the apostles and the believers who were in Judea heard that the Gentiles had also accepted the word of God. So when Peter went up to Jerusalem, the circumcised believers criticised him, saying, 'Why did you go to uncircumcised men and eat with them?' Then Peter began to explain… 'I was in the city of Joppa praying, and in a trance I saw a vision. There was something like a large sheet coming down from heaven, being lowered by its four corners… As I looked at it closely I saw four-footed animals, beasts of prey, reptiles, and birds of the air. I also heard a voice saying to me, 'Get up, Peter; kill and eat.' But I replied, 'By no means, Lord; for nothing profane or unclean has ever entered my mouth.' But a second time the voice answered from heaven, 'What God has made clean, you must not call profane.' This happened three times; then everything was pulled up again to heaven. At that very moment three men, sent to me from Caesarea, arrived at the house where we were. The Spirit told me to go with them and not to make a distinction between them and us…

'And as I began to speak, the Holy Spirit fell upon them just as it had upon us at the beginning… If then God gave them the same gift that he gave us when we believed in the Lord Jesus Christ, who was I that I could hinder God?' When they heard this, they were silenced. And then they praised God, saying, 'Then God has given even to the Gentiles the repentance that leads to life.'

ACTS 11:1–12, 15, 17–18 (ABRIDGED)

We began our journey this Lent a long way from home, in the company of the prodigal son in 'a distant country', and of Jacob, who cheated his twin Esau out of his birthright and their father Isaac's blessing. From those places of alienation and isolation, we began to catch glimpses of a wonderful and mysterious truth—that the loving God who formed us in the womb (Psalm 139) seeks to draw us, in spite of our sin and from however far we may have travelled, back into the warmth of his loving embrace. On the threshold of Week 1, we stood with Christ at his baptism, hearing the assurance that we are, indeed, God's beloved children.

Since those early days we have journeyed with Christ into the temptations in the desert; we have undertaken some explorations down the ancient pathways of prayer and have been encouraged to enjoy with gratitude the various 'oases of welcome' our lives have offered. Strengthened by these loving gifts, we have also sought the courage to encounter aspects of the shadow side of our human nature.

As our spiritual journey deepens, we are faced with the same kind of challenge that faced the early Christians—to resist the ever-present temptation to put God into a box, attempting to confine him to a place in our thinking and lives that gives us the illusion of security and safety. We tend to prefer to stay with what we know, but God constantly challenges us to allow him to stretch and transcend our boundaries. As the American poet Minnie Louise Haskins expressed it, 'Step out into the darkness and put your hand into the hand of God. That shall be to you better than light, and safer than a known way.'[67]

As we consider Peter's vision concerning the 'clean' and 'unclean' animals, we join the narrative at a point where the fledgling Christian church is being coaxed into taking a quantum leap forward in its understanding of the ways of God. Proud of their heritage and conscious of their destiny as God's chosen people, the idea that God was using the believers as a channel of his love to the Gentiles was deeply unsettling, despite the hints embedded in Israel's own history (see Genesis 17:4–7; Joshua 5:13–14; Isaiah 52:10; Luke 2:29–32).

Something of the disciples' confusion and uncertainty is reflected in the opening verses of our passage. To the consternation of many, it was becoming clear that the gift of the Holy Spirit was not reserved for 'circumcised believers' alone, but that Gentiles also (of whom Cornelius the centurion has already been introduced as a shining example, in Acts 10:1–8) were being equally blessed (11:1). Even Peter, despite living and working so closely with Jesus, was resistant to this development, and yet his cooperation in this venture was vital. As the American theologian Robert W. Wall bluntly expresses it, 'God's redemptive purposes for Gentiles could not be realised unless the apostle changed his mind.'[68] Peter, in this passage, is facing the suspicion and accusations of his fellow believers as he explains to them that the triple repetition within his vision finally jolted his understanding to a new level.

The difficulty that Peter and his fellow believers experienced may be a familiar one. The fact that we know we are special to God and are deeply loved by him is a wonderful gift, but it carries with it the danger that we may come to view ourselves as somehow more special, or more privileged, than others. Robert W. Wall writes, 'Those believers who think themselves among God's "elect" are often inclined on this theological basis to think that God has not chosen anyone else who disagrees with their beliefs and customs.'[69] We have seen the global fall-out from this thinking, throughout history and down to the present day—from Crusades, burning in the name of religion, the unimaginable evil of the holocaust and ethnic cleansings the world over, to the horrors of 9/11. But fear of the unknown also constrains and restricts us far more immediately—from our reactions to those whom we perceive as 'outsiders' in our communities to the endless bickering and defensiveness clustering around whatever are the current disagreements within our churches. We have a long way to go before we can confidently say with Peter; 'I truly understand that God shows no partiality, but in every nation anyone who fears him and does what is right is acceptable to him' (Acts 10:34–35).

For reflection and prayer

'I am the good shepherd. I know my own and my own know me... I have other sheep that do not belong to this fold. I must bring them also, and they will listen to my voice.

JOHN 10:14, 16

A question

'I truly understand that God shows no partiality' (Acts 10:34). To what extent is this true in the life of your own church?

Monday

Hearing and responding

Then an angel of the Lord said to Philip, 'Get up and go towards the south to the road that goes down from Jerusalem to Gaza.' (This is a wilderness road.) So he got up and went. Now there was an Ethiopian eunuch, a court official of the Candace, queen of the Ethiopians, in charge of her entire treasury. He had come to Jerusalem to worship and was returning home; seated in his chariot, he was reading the prophet Isaiah. Then the Spirit said to Philip, 'Go over to this chariot and join it.' So Philip ran up to it and heard him reading the prophet Isaiah. He asked, 'Do you understand what you are reading?' He replied, 'How can I, unless someone guides me?' And he invited Philip to get in and sit beside him...

Then Philip began to speak, and starting with this scripture, he proclaimed to him the good news about Jesus. As they were going along the road, they came to some water; and the eunuch said, 'Look, here is water! What is to prevent me from being baptised?' He commanded the chariot to stop, and both of them, Philip and the eunuch, went down into the water, and Philip baptised him. When they came up out of the water, the Spirit of the Lord snatched Philip away; the eunuch saw him no more, and went on his way rejoicing.

ACTS 8:26–31, 35–39

We have been considering God's call to the early church to allow its boundaries to be extended beyond the Jewish nation. Luke approaches this watershed moment from several angles. Yesterday we witnessed Peter take an immense step of imaginative faith and obedience as he was able to welcome the messengers of Cornelius, a Gentile God-fearer from outside the boundaries of the chosen people. Today we accompany Philip, who, along with the first Christian martyr, Stephen, had been one of the group of seven deacons chosen to serve the church in Jerusalem, in order that the twelve apostles could be set free for the work of prayer and teaching (Acts 6:1–6).

After the martyrdom of Stephen, the church was subject to severe persecution (7:1—8:1), and all the disciples except the Jerusalem apostles were scattered throughout Judea and Samaria. Philip has just come to the end of what seems to have been a highly successful mission in Samaria (8:4–8). We join him as he obeys the direction of an angel of the Lord and goes immediately to the road from Jerusalem to Gaza.

The Ethiopian eunuch is an intriguing character. The term 'eunuch' (in Hebrew, *saris*) had two meanings, the primary meaning referring to a court officer or official, and the secondary sense to a castrated male. The term, when used, didn't necessarily embody both meanings; someone could be a court officer without being a castrate (as in the case of Potiphar, who had a wife: Genesis 39:7), while, in the reference in Isaiah 56:3, the secondary meaning is clear. Our Ethiopian eunuch clearly fulfils the first criterion: as the court official in charge of the treasury of the queen, he was obviously held in very high regard and his status would have been considerable. It is not clear from today's text whether he also fulfilled the second definition of the term.

Philip discovers the eunuch on the road and, at the Spirit's direction, approaches his chariot. The Ethiopian is clearly a God-seeker: we are told that he is reading the prophet Isaiah; he has been to Jerusalem to worship and is now returning home. If the Ethiopian eunuch was a castrate as well as a high-ranking official, this visit to Jerusalem could have aggravated the evolving religious situation for the Jewish people. Castration (along with other varieties of physical impairment) barred the sufferer from participation in temple worship, with restoration to full fellowship only possible in the event of a healing[70]—despite the prophecy of Isaiah which had long ago urged the people to 'maintain justice, and do what is right' (56:1) and declared God's promise 'to the eunuchs who keep my sabbaths, who choose the things that please me... I will give them an everlasting name that shall not be cut off' (vv. 4–5).

Another interesting aspect of this passage is to be found in Philip's response to the divine prompting and a comparison of his response with that of Peter in yesterday's text. At every stage in this narrative, Philip is described as responding immediately and without question to the divine imperative: 'An angel of the Lord said to Philip, "Get up and go..." So he got up and went' (vv. 26–27). When instructed by the Spirit to approach the chariot, 'Philip ran up to it and heard [the Ethiopian] reading the prophet Isaiah' (v. 30). There is no doubt or hesitation here: Philip jumps rapidly and immediately into action.

What a contrast with Peter! Three times the large sheet in his vision containing the animals and birds was lowered in front of him, and three times he refused to obey the divine injunction to kill and eat: 'By no means, Lord; for I have never eaten anything that is profane or unclean' (10:14). For

Peter, the meaning of the vision became clear only with the actual arrival of the three men sent by Cornelius, when he was finally able to obey.

It was with good reason that Jesus urged his disciples to travel light (Matthew 10:9–10), avoiding the temptation to encumber themselves with unnecessary baggage, but it is entirely possible that some of the goods with which we weigh ourselves down may not be material things at all. Sometimes it may be our religious and spiritual practices that get in the way. Philip seems to have been able to travel around unencumbered, free from anxiety and able to move where the Spirit led him, whereas Peter's perception of himself as a good and upright Jew initially prevented him from responding even to the voice of the Lord.

For reflection and prayer

John said to [Jesus], 'Teacher, we saw someone casting out demons in your name, and we tried to stop him, because he was not following us.' But Jesus said, 'Do not stop him; for no one who does a deed of power in my name will be able soon afterwards to speak evil of me. Whoever is not against us is for us.'

MARK 9:38–40

A question

Philip seems to have travelled around unencumbered. Are we free enough from 'excess baggage' to be able to move where the Spirit may lead?

Tuesday

A welcome for all

'But I say to you that listen, Love your enemies, do good to those who hate you, bless those who curse you, pray for those who abuse you. If anyone strikes you on the cheek, offer the other also; and from anyone who takes away your coat do not withhold even your shirt. Give to everyone who begs from you; and if anyone takes away your goods, do not ask for them again. Do to others as you would have them do to you. If you love those who love you, what credit is that to you? For even sinners love those who love them... But love your enemies, do good, and lend, expecting nothing in return... Be merciful, just as your Father is merciful.'
LUKE 6:27–32, 35–36 (ABRIDGED)

Today's reading is a small section of the Sermon on the Plain (Luke 6:17–49), in which Jesus lays out a pattern for generous living to Christians who are living in a largely hostile world. The bracing challenge of his words hits us (if we allow it) like a shock of cold water: 'Love your enemies, do good to those who hate you, bless those who curse you, pray for those who abuse you' (vv. 27–28). We may try to rationalise and soften the impact of Christ's words: did he *really* mean these words as they read to us? Of course, we say, we live in a very different world, and things are not as clear-cut and straightforward now...

But a moment's further reflection reveals to us the basic

problem with this response. The world itself may have changed in a multitude of ways but human nature itself has not changed: humanity still struggles with the same tendencies to greed, possessiveness, pride, envy and suspicion of others as it always did. We may protest that this teaching is too idealistic: how is it possible for anyone to love in the way Jesus commands? We love our families, our neighbours and our friends: isn't that as much as we can be expected to manage? This must also have been the reaction of Jesus' original hearers, and his response to them is also his response to our protests: 'If you love those who love you, what credit is that to you? For even sinners love those who love them' (v. 32). There is no 'letting off the hook' for disciples, either then or now.

The potential stumbling block of this passage lies particularly in the first few verses ('If anyone strikes you on the cheek...' through to '... do not ask for them again', vv. 29–30). These words raise a valid and urgent question: doesn't the attitude demanded here encourage a passive response to violence and evil? There is no easy answer, and on the occasion(s) of the cleansing of the temple even Jesus responded with anger and a degree of violence (Matthew 21:12–13; John 2:13–16). So whatever else this teaching is about, it is not about simply standing by and passively accepting the status quo.

The key to our understanding and interpretation of this passage lies in its opening words: 'But I say *to you that listen*...' Jesus is speaking to those who are already disciples (vv. 17, 20), who have already heard the beatitudes and the woes (vv. 20–26) and are already—potentially at least—in possession of God's kingdom (v. 20). In the words of the American New Testament scholar Susan E. Hylen, 'The knowledge that "yours is the kingdom of God" transforms the disciple's actions from compliance to resistance in the face of evil.'[71] Jesus is giving his followers a dramatic new frame of reference: they may be viewed with suspicion or even outright hostility by those around them, but from the perspective of the kingdom the despised disciple is truly 'blessed'. This runs totally counter to the world's understanding, but an ability to accept this radical spiritual truth enables the believer to share in the authority of God's kingdom. The knowledge that we are deeply loved by God and are cherished children of his kingdom therefore creates in us a potential to respond to others in generosity and love—even when those sentiments are not reciprocated. Susan Hylen continues:

> When the teachings of the Sermon on the Plain are not grounded in the disciple's identity as God's child, they become an onerous list of ethical demands that do not further justice and wholeness. When the disciple understands his actions as flowing out of God's abundance, to which he belongs and which belongs to him, turning the other cheek becomes an act of resistance to evil that has the power to transform others and the world.[72]

We extend hospitality to others, friends and foes alike, when we offer them acceptance and welcome; we need also to be able to extend such hospitality to ourselves. In their book *Radical Hospitality*, Daniel Homan and Lonni Collins Pratt state, 'Our ability to accept others begins with whether or not we are in touch with our dark side.'[73] Psychological developments over the past century have shown just how vulnerable we are in this respect. As Homan and Pratt indicate, if we cannot honestly own and accept the negative aspects of our own personality, we are likely to project those negative aspects outwards into other people and situations. The resulting poison injected into the community through our lack of self-awareness contributes to and enlarges the conflicts and dis-ease in society as a whole.

We have met the Carmelite nun Ruth Burrows earlier in our Lenten journey (Wednesday, Week 1), with her teaching that we need to be patient with ourselves and be 'content to see the smears of self'.[74] This is not complacency; rather, it acknowledges the need for us to recognise and accept our human weakness and fallibility. We cannot 'put ourselves right'; only Christ can bring about our lifelong healing and transformation. As far as generous hospitality is concerned, looking outwards and looking inwards are two sides of the same coin, and both aspects provide us with a lifetime of challenge. In the words of Homan and Pratt, 'Hospitality, rather than being something you achieve, is something you enter. It is an adventure that takes you where you never dreamed of going. It is not something you do, as much as it is someone you become.'[75]

For reflection and prayer

Let mutual love continue. Do not neglect to show hospitality to strangers, for by doing that some have entertained angels without knowing it.

HEBREWS 13:1–2

A question

Did Christ really mean his words in Luke 6? If so, what might they mean for our lives now?

Wednesday

Two by two

After this the Lord appointed seventy others and sent them on ahead of him in pairs to every town and place where he himself intended to go. He said to them, 'The harvest is plentiful, but the labourers are few; therefore ask the Lord of the harvest to send out labourers into his harvest. Go on your way. See, I am sending you out like lambs into the midst of wolves.'

LUKE 10:1–3

Both the pace of events and the pressure on Jesus are intensifying. The passage immediately before these verses from Luke indicate that the time for active ministry is drawing to a close and the days are drawing near for him 'to be taken up' (9:51). As he prepares to go to Jerusalem, he sends messengers on ahead, but their approaches are rejected. The mission of the 70, which begins with today's verses, takes place after this initial rejection, after which Jesus spells out yet again just how costly and difficult the life of the disciple will inevitably be (9:57–62).

Jesus then sends the 70 disciples out in pairs 'to every town and place where he himself intended to go' (10:1). There is an interesting difference from the earlier sending out (9:52) in the fact that the disciples are now to travel in pairs. The earlier rejection will have highlighted again both the enormity of the task ('The harvest is plentiful, but the labourers are few, 10:2) and the vulnerability of those who are sent out into, effectively, enemy territory ('See, I am sending you out like lambs into the midst of wolves', v. 3).

Clearly, much has changed across the intervening centuries, but Jesus' commission to his followers today is essentially the same. Our society, with its secularism and rampant consumerism, is still apparently deaf to and, at times, actively hostile to the gospel of Christ. The task for Christ's followers is still enormous and disciples will still be vulnerable, but we should take encouragement from the fact that now, as then, it is God who is responsible for the growth and change in our communities. Our task is to be open to that potential for growth and to work in such a way that we assist and cooperate with God's purposes rather than hinder and obstruct them.

On this last point, it is significant that Jesus sends out his disciples in pairs. Where there are two and one has lost heart, the other is there for encouragement. Where one loses sight of the goal ahead, the other may be able to help resharpen the vision, and, in the unavoidable vulnerability of those called to be Christ's disciples, the company of another can act as a channel of God's strength and protection.

The church was not slow to appreciate the value of such a practice, and, from the time of the desert tradition onwards, the practice of spiritual accompaniment, or direction, has been encouraged. The roots of the tradition lie in Jesus and his relationship as rabbi-teacher to his disciples, and there are numerous examples of individual and group 'spiritual direction' in the Gospels (John 3:1–21; Luke 22:24–27; Matthew 6—7; the parables). As an aid to personal and spiritual growth and development, the tradition has evolved over the centuries in both Christianity and in other faiths, with the director being known by a variety of names according to time, historical circumstance and balance between the parties in the relationship. The Celtic tradition speaks of an *anamcara*, or soul-friend; the Russian Orthodox Church has the *starets* and the Buddhist faith has the *roshi*.

For much of the last 2000 years, the direction relationship has been an unequal one, and the disciple in earlier periods was expected to respond to the director with complete obedience, acknowledging the director's greater knowledge and experience. For most of history, the giving of spiritual direction was almost totally the province of the clergy or of men and women in religious orders, but, over the last 100 years or so, it is a ministry in which lay people also have become increasingly involved. The spiritual direction relationship today tends to be a little more relaxed, with the terms 'spiritual accompaniment' or 'soul friend' reflecting the shift in emphasis. But whatever the particular circumstances and terminology used, the essential constituents of support, encouragement and guidance have remained constant in every generation.

Christian people today might seek such a relationship for a number of reasons. For the disciple at the beginning of their spiritual journey, such guidance and support can be invaluable, and many churches today offer a form of something similar within 'mentoring' schemes. Here, a person preparing for baptism and/or confirmation is paired with a more experienced member of the fellowship for encouragement and support. A person might seek such support as their faith begins to grow or when finding themselves questioning that faith (which can itself be a sign of growth). For others, the catalyst may be some kind of life crisis, such as marriage or bereavement, divorce, childbirth or redundancy.

We have been reflecting today on the two areas of mission and spiritual accompaniment, and at first sight there may not appear to be much of a connection between them, but the connection is there, and it is a deep one. The common root is to be found in Jesus and his intimate relationship with his disciples, both in his own time and through all the ages since. We see the connection when Jesus teaches, as in the parables; when he challenges, as on the occasions when earthly praise and reward supplant the values of the kingdom; when he encourages, at those times when we are disheartened and dispirited by the reality of our human frailty. In his working with us in all this through the love and support of one another, Christ sends us out into the harvest to share in his mission for the world.

For reflection and prayer

Two are better than one, because they have a good reward for their toil. For if they fall, one will lift up the other; but woe to the one who is alone and falls and does not have another to help.

ECCLESIASTES 4:9–10

A question

Have you ever considered seeking spiritual direction? Might this be something that could help and support you on your spiritual journey?

Thursday

Living in the wilderness

'And you, child, will be called the prophet of the Most High; for you will go before the Lord to prepare his ways, to give knowledge of salvation to his people by the forgiveness of their sins. By the tender mercy of our God, the dawn from on high will break upon us, to give light to those who sit in darkness and in the shadow of death, to guide our feet into the way of peace.' The child grew and became strong in spirit, and he was in the wilderness until the day he appeared publicly to Israel.

LUKE 1:76–80

Biblical commentaries on the Gospels rightly devote a great deal of energy and attention to the magnificent hymn known as the Benedictus (Luke 1:68–79). Since the angel's foretelling of the birth of John the Baptist (vv. 8–20), Zechariah had been struck dumb on account of his questioning of the angel's message. At this point in the narrative his tongue is released, and this hymn is the form taken by Zechariah's outpouring of prophecy and praise on the birth of his son. The passage concludes with a reference to the growing spiritual strength of the child John, together with the enigmatic comment that 'he was in the wilderness until the day he appeared publicly to Israel' (v. 80). It is puzzling that many commentaries simply pass over this statement, moving directly from the close of the Benedictus to the decree sent out from Caesar Augustus in 2:1.

Why this silence? Could part of the reason be that, as 21st-century Christians, we have no real concept of what a vocation to 'live in the desert' might mean? Earlier centuries do not seem to have had the same difficulty: to them, the reference to John the Baptist's early years in the desert carries no sense of strangeness or peculiarity, and we saw in Week 1 that in the early Christian centuries it was far from unusual to live out one's vocation as a solitary, or hermit, in a desert context. Nor was the recognition of this calling confined to the early centuries. Across Europe in the Middle Ages, men sought to live as hermits, living a simple life of prayer outside the monasteries. Some moved from place to place; others settled on the edges of villages and towns and carried out work for the community, such as road-mending, bridge-building or, in a few cases, lighthouse-keeping.

Medieval women were not free to travel in the same way and were frequently drawn to live out a solitary vocation of prayer and contemplation as 'anchoresses'. These women were not necessarily members of religious orders but sought to live out their lives as Christian solitaries within their communities. Under the authority of the local bishop, their 'desert' generally took the form of a simple cell, physically attached or 'anchored' to the wall of the local parish church. Following the desert tradition, the anchoress would live, pray and perhaps engage in simple manual work such as sewing, with a maid to attend to her practical needs. There would be two windows in the cell, one facing into the church, enabling the anchoress to hear Mass and receive Communion, and the other facing out, so that local people could visit her for spiritual counsel and advice. One of the most famous anchoresses, from the 14th century, was Julian of Norwich.

Fourteenth-century England had no problem with the Christian call to the solitary life; it was a universally recognised and highly respected element of the kaleidoscope of vocations that made up medieval church life. Then, through the complex process that was the European Reformation, perceptions changed. Our church life today seems to be more about 'doing' than about 'being', and those perceived to be the most committed Christians tend to be those who are most visibly active. Even in the 21st century, though, God still calls people to the solitary life—across the world, in literal deserts or hidden within villages, towns and cities. Some are members of religious orders but many are not: they may be male or female, married or single and at different stages of life. The solitary calling may have emerged initially through a life-crisis such as bereavement, retirement or redundancy, or it may have arisen through a gradually unfolding sense of inner conviction that God's primary call to the person is one of prayer.

The call may initially have been difficult to hear, as it runs counter to the expectations of most local church communities, in which active involvement is the norm and contemplative prayer is seen as the domain of those who are too old or sick to do anything more 'useful'. The present-day solitary Eve Baker explains:

Because this call is not generally understood today it can be the cause of distress. Anyone who chooses to be alone is seen to be 'opting out', whether from the usual social occasions or from the present-day Christian scene where the norm is to be involved, to be ministering to others and to be seen to be ministering. Anyone not so involved is regarded as odd, deviant or defective.[76]

Part of the problem for members of today's church is that we have lost that medieval sense of the solitary vocation as holding a legitimate place within the whole body of Christ, along with all the other more 'active' vocations. Eve Baker counters our present-day misunderstanding quite bluntly: 'The Christian solitary exists within the Church, the company of the baptised, and the solitary vocation must be lived out in dialogue with the Christian tradition... It is a gift to the whole Church, a sign of the transcendence of God.'[77]

Tomorrow we will consider how this vocation may be a gift to the church and a sign of God's transcendence, and reflect on some of the ways in which the life and vocation of the solitary may develop.

For reflection and prayer

O God, you are my God, I seek you, my soul thirsts for you; my flesh faints for you, as in a dry and weary land where there is no water.

PSALM 63:1

A question

Can you identify any ways in which the solitary experience is the lot of every human being?

Friday

The fruits of solitude

Rejoice always, pray without ceasing, give thanks in all circumstances; for this is the will of God in Christ Jesus for you... May the God of peace himself sanctify you entirely.
1 THESSALONIANS 5:16–18, 23

One of the many criticisms directed at those who sense they may have a solitary vocation is that such a way of life is self-centred, unconcerned with the 'real' work of ministry and mission in which the church seeks to engage and involve its members. Yet Paul's exhortation to 'pray without ceasing', aimed here at the whole Christian community, is a keystone of the life of the solitary. Solitaries have always been misunderstood, being seen as having placed themselves outside the boundaries of the church, concerned only with 'doing their own thing'. For those who think in this way, Eve Baker's statement (which we read yesterday) concerning the place of the solitary within the church as a gift and a sign of God's transcendence, poses something of a challenge.

How might such a vocation be a 'gift' to the church? I am reminded of the prophet Jeremiah, who was at times asked by God to act out a visual parable that would dramatically convey God's message to the people (see, for example, Jeremiah 13 and 19). The solitary is not 'acting' as such, but there is a sense in which the solitary's presence within a highly active Christian community can serve as a reminder to all that their primary calling is one of prayer and a deepening relationship with God. Thomas Merton expresses a similar sentiment when he writes of the relationship of the solitary to the wider context of society: 'The true solitary is not one who simply withdraws from society. Mere withdrawal, regression, leads to a sick solitude, without meaning and without fruit. The solitary of whom I speak is called not to leave society but to transcend it.'[78]

This is all very well, but how may a person who is called by God into a deeper solitude within the body of Christ recognise such a call? Such people will almost certainly experience strong resistance from at least two directions—from their particular church community and from within themselves. The first of these we have already touched upon. We saw earlier how strong and vocal were Martha's complaints to Jesus, as her sister Mary sat quietly at Jesus' feet listening to him, and there will be many good Christian people who respond similarly to the perceived 'idleness' of the solitary in their midst. In defence of the one truly called by God in this way, Jesus' response is exactly the same: 'Martha, Martha, you are worried and distracted by many things; there is need of only one thing. Mary has chosen the better part, which will not be taken away from her.' (Luke 10:41–42).

Potential solitaries will almost certainly experience a resistance from within themselves, however. We are children of a society that strives for more, bigger and better, and where visible activity and success are prized above all else. For the solitary, the still, small voice of God intrudes into all this activity and outward striving, calling the person deeper, to the source of the living waters. Such a call may well mean letting go of other activities, good in themselves, which would get in the way of the primary task of the solitary—prayer.

It is here that we need to confront another common misunderstanding, the same one into which Martha fell—that the solitary is not doing anything of any 'use' at all. But what Martha missed, and what our busy, often over-active churches continue to miss, is a remarkable paradox, expressed very clearly by Eve Baker: 'The life of the solitary is a silent and hidden life which grows within the busy demanding everyday life we all lead.'[79]

Baker is saying that the solitary life grows within the circumstances of daily life, not at a distance from them. The place where the solitary happens to be located—in the desert or in the city—is not the primary concern. How can this be possible?

As mentioned yesterday, there are many hermits and solitaries living hidden lives of prayer today; some in situations of actual solitude but others in the midst of family and work responsibilities. One of the most well-known of the latter was Catherine de Hueck Doherty (1896–1985), a Russian aristocrat who had narrowly escaped death at the hands of the Bolsheviks during the Revolution. A deeply committed Catholic Christian, she forged a new life for herself in America; there she founded Friendship House, serving the poor and marginalised through centres in a number of cities. In the midst of a hugely busy and demanding life, she developed and taught the vital importance of *poustinia*, a Russian term meaning 'desert'. Juggling the responsibilities of marriage and family and the work of Friendship House with a growing sense of a call to solitude, she saw these apparently competing demands not as mutually exclusive but as complementary, to be held in balance with each other. If that balance could be maintained by the solitary, then the effects could be far-reaching:

The poustinia is a state of constantly being in the presence of God because one desires him with a great desire, because in him alone can one rest. The poustinia is walking in this inner solitude, immersed in the silence of God. My life of service and love to my fellowman is simply the echo of this silence and solitude.[80]

For us in today's church, of whatever denomination, there is great encouragement here. Doherty's experience urges us to respond to the call to solitude, not necessarily beyond the current boundaries of our lives, but within them. She stresses that deserts and solitudes 'are not necessarily places but states of mind and heart', and continues:

These deserts can be found in the midst of the city, and in the everyday of our lives... They will be small solitudes, little deserts, tiny pools of silence, but the experience they will bring, if we are disposed to enter them, may be as exultant and holy as all the deserts of the world, even the one God himself entered. For it is God who makes solitude, deserts and silences holy.[81]

For reflection and prayer

[The Lord] sustained [Jacob] in a desert land, in a howling wilderness waste; he shielded him, cared for him, guarded him as the apple of his eye.

DEUTERONOMY 32:10

A question

Thomas Merton wrote, 'The solitary of whom I speak is called not to leave society but to transcend it.' What do you think he meant by this?

Saturday

Balance of life

For everything there is a season, and a time for every matter under heaven: a time to be born, and a time to die; a time to plant, and a time to pluck up what is planted; a time to kill, and a time to heal; a time to break down, and a time to build up; a time to weep, and a time to laugh; a time to mourn, and a time to dance; a time to throw away stones, and a time to gather stones together; a time to embrace, and a time to refrain from embracing; a time to seek, and a time to lose; a time to keep, and a tim e to throw away; a time to tear, and a time to sew; a time to keep silence, and a time to speak; a time to love, and a time to hate; a time for war, and a time for peace.

ECCLESIASTES 3:1–8

For many who were young people in the mid-1960s, these memorable verses became universally popular as the number one hit 'Turn! Turn! Turn!' (1965) by the American folk rock band The Byrds. The words were taken almost verbatim from the King James Version of the book of Ecclesiastes, although the sequence of the phrases was rearranged. Theological study over many years has yielded many possible interpretations for these words but, in the song, they were intended as a plea for world peace.

Yet this admirable sentiment does pose a problematic question for the disciple. 'A plea for world peace,' says the song writer—but 'a time to kill' (v. 3), 'a time to hate' and 'a time of war' (v. 8) are as much a part of the verses' total pattern as are their opposites. Is there not a contradiction here? Some biblical scholars have stumbled over the apparently fixed nature of the scheme: if all these actions and experiences are in some way predestined, what is the responsibility of human beings in them? Where is the place for conscience and moral action? What is the point of offering a plea for world peace if war is an inevitable part of the pattern? The author of Ecclesiastes takes a somewhat jaundiced view of life and faith, where 'all is vanity and a chasing after wind' (2:17). Seen within this context, his poem does indeed adopt a bleak and pessimistic outlook.

The American Biblical scholar W. Sibley Towner suggests a possible way out of the impasse. He observes that commentators and preachers alike have not wanted to confine this beautiful poem within the somewhat grim prison of predetermination. Turning against the approach of most biblical criticism in this instance, Towner invites the reader to consider the poem independently of its context of predeterminism. If we are able to do this, a refreshingly different emphasis emerges. Towner writes:

If one reads the poem with the understanding that the fixed orders provide structure rather than calendar, then individual human moral decision making is possible. One can then hear in this poem a challenge to be wise, to be ethical, to discern when one's actions are in keeping with God's time and then to act decisively.[82]

It is also true to say that the sentiments and experiences named in this passage accurately reflect the reality of life in a fallen world. Jesus once said to his hearers, 'You always have the poor with you' (Mark 14:7). The references to death, hatred and war in this poem reflect the same fallen reality, but it does not necessarily follow that we should make no effort to exercise our consciences or to do what we can to relieve suffering wherever and whenever possible.

There is more here that can both nourish and challenge us. We met the Swiss psychologist and psychiatrist Carl Jung earlier (Sunday, Week 4). His important paper entitled 'The Stages of Life' (1930)[83] addresses in broad terms the tasks and general direction of the two major life phases. The first part, life's morning, is chiefly concerned with the outward journey into the world—physical growth and development, education, work and family—but the emphasis changes with the second part, life's afternoon/evening. Here the journey becomes, and needs to become, more inward. Physically the body is moving towards its death, and many of the outer experiences of life in this stage give a foretaste of it—illness, retirement, bereavement. As in our poem from Ecclesiastes, the path of wisdom lies in accepting the pattern: we cannot change it, for all our desperate efforts with cosmetic surgery, and Jung has a terrible warning for those who try.

We cannot live the afternoon of life according to the pattern of life's morning; for what was great in the morning will be little at evening, and what in the morning was true will at evening have become a lie. I have given psychological treatment to too many people of advancing years… not to be moved by this fundamental truth.[84]

A few weeks ago (Sunday, Week 3) we reflected on Hildegard of Bingen's wonderful vision 'The circle of life', with its graphic representations of the seasons, each giving way to the next, and the accompanying rhythm and pattern of humanity's toil and rest. 'Turn! Turn! Turn!' The repeated words making up the title of the 1965 pop song are not found in the biblical poem but they reflect the pattern, capturing the essence of these verses from Ecclesiastes perfectly. The rhythmic repetition of the short phrase 'A time to...' (if we can accept the pattern and the inevitability of our changing place within it) creates a feeling of stability, inner peace and belonging. The experience of death is an integral part of the whole, and perhaps this is one of the biggest elements of the cross that we are invited to welcome. Every feeling and experience has its due and rightful place in the ordered pattern of life and we are challenged to embrace the whole.

For reflection and prayer

But I trust in you, O Lord; I say, 'You are my God.' My times are in your hand... Be strong, and let your heart take courage, all you who wait for the Lord.

PSALM 31:14–15a, 24

A question

We may assent to the psalmist's declaration, 'You are my God. My times are in your hand.' Do we also agree with it in our hearts, when we consider the reality of our present life experience?

Holy Week

Open to the cross

Palm Sunday

Praise and welcome

When [Jesus] had come near Bethphage and Bethany, at the place called the Mount of Olives, he sent two of the disciples, saying, 'Go into the village ahead of you, and as you enter it you will find tied there a colt that has never been ridden. Untie it and bring it here. If anyone asks you, "Why are you untying it?" just say this: "The Lord needs it."' So those who were sent departed and found it as he had told them. As they were untying the colt, its owners asked them, 'Why are you untying the colt?' They said, 'The Lord needs it.' Then they brought it to Jesus; and after throwing their cloaks on the colt, they set Jesus on it. As he rode along, people kept spreading their cloaks on the road. As he was now approaching the path down from the Mount of Olives, the whole multitude of the disciples began to praise God joyfully with a loud voice for all the deeds of power that they had seen, saying, 'Blessed is the king who comes in the name of the Lord! Peace in heaven, and glory in the highest heaven!'
LUKE 19:29–38

As I write today's reflection, the long wait is finally over. Supporters and enthusiasts have been vindicated and the critics have been silenced (for the moment); last-minute glitches appear to have been overcome and the eagerly anticipated 2012 London Olympic Games have just got under way. Witnessed by thousands in the main Olympic arena and many millions more on television, the lighting of the Olympic flame proved a fitting climax to an opening ceremony that delighted and dazzled in equal measure.

The spectacular fireworks of the Games' opening were preceded by something equally impressive—the 70-day odyssey of the Olympic flame after it arrived on our shores at Land's End and then travelled across the length and breadth of the British Isles on its way to London. Each day, the progress of the flame was eagerly charted and, in each community that the torch passed through, people turned out in their hundreds and thousands to cheer it on. The journalist India Hicks wrote powerfully of its effect:

Last Thursday the torch finally arrived in my bit of London. It was 6.30am and I thought there would maybe be 200 people watching, most of them children and pensioners. How wrong I was: the streets were crammed with thousands of people of all ages… We cheered ourselves hoarse and I wanted to cry.

Hicks goes on to write of the miraculously transforming effect on people who were living in an area that had been one of the 'hotspots' of the London riots: 'Everyone was beaming, chatting to one another, wishing one another a nice day and a good summer.'[85]

Hicks may have joined the crowd welcoming the torch relay with only moderate expectations, but the crowd who welcomed Jesus on his entry into Jerusalem were riding high on a crest of hope and euphoria. The news about Jesus, his teaching and his healings had been spreading like wildfire, culminating in this highly charged moment of longing and expectation when the people's hope of a national saviour appeared to be on the brink of fulfilment. But the problem with this joy-filled welcome was that it also indicated the limits of the crowd's thinking about Jesus. Their suffering was over; this was the moment when Christ was going to liberate their country! Even after the resurrection, Jesus' closest disciples found it difficult to think 'outside the box' as they asked him, 'Lord, is this the time when you will restore the kingdom to Israel?' (Acts 1:6). Even after three years of living and working in close proximity to Jesus, those closest to him were seemingly unable to see that his goal was far, far greater than simply one nation's liberation.

When Jesus made his triumphal entry into Jerusalem, the crowd had no foreknowledge of the tragic conclusion of the coming week's events, or of how rapidly their mood would change from 'Hosanna!' to 'Crucify!' as they realised that their nationalistic expectations were not to be fulfilled. The American theologian R. Alan Culpepper describes Jesus' entry into Jerusalem as 'a moment filled with fragile possibility'[86] concealing the seeds of so many future 'if onlys'. If only Jesus had seized the moment... If only the religious leaders had had a deeper perception of what was really happening in front of their eyes... If only the people of Jerusalem had responded as they should...! We may well be able to identify with some of these reactions; most of our lives are strewn with plans that did not materialise and situations in which everything seemed just right but somehow didn't work out as we had hoped. It is in this common human experience that we encounter a tricky question: how able are we in our discipleship to allow God to be God? How well can we accept with inner peace the fact that his ways are not our ways, or his thoughts our thoughts? Do we more usually react with disappointment and dismay when we don't understand and our desires appear to have been frustrated?

If we are seeking to be open to the way of the cross, we will find ourselves increasingly challenged to stand apart from the crowd and take a longer, deeper view. The true goal, embodied in Jesus as he entered Jerusalem, may not be immediately apparent to those of us experiencing the event. Sometimes, as with the Olympic torch relay, the mood of the crowd is positive and joyful and builds up its participants; on other occasions, as in the case of the London riots, the mood may turn ugly and sway the participants in an altogether less positive direction. Whether the mood tends towards good or evil, we are encouraged to exercise our personal discernment and judgment, and resist the temptation to be wholly sucked in. We need to seek a deeper wisdom than that of the crowd.

For reflection and prayer

'And now, O Lord my God... Give your servant... an understanding mind... able to discern between good and evil.'
1 KINGS 3:7, 9 (ABRIDGED)

Monday

With one heart
and mind

Six days before the Passover Jesus came to Bethany, the home of Lazarus, whom he had raised from the dead. There they gave a dinner for him. Martha served, and Lazarus was one of those at table with him. Mary took a pound of costly perfume made of pure nard, anointed Jesus' feet, and wiped them with her hair. The house was filled with the fragrance of the perfume. But Judas Iscariot, one of the disciples (the one who was about to betray him), said, 'Why was this perfume not sold for three hundred denarii and the money given to the poor? (He said this not because he cared about the poor, but because he was a thief; he kept the common purse and used to steal what was put into it.) Jesus said, 'Leave her alone. She bought it so that she might keep it for the day of my burial. You always have the poor with you, but you do not always have me.'

JOHN 12:1–8

The home of his friends Mary, Martha and Lazarus had long provided a safe haven of love, security and friendship for Jesus amid the pressure of his public ministry. Today's reading describes a dinner that has been held in Jesus' honour, probably in thanksgiving and celebration after his raising of Lazarus from the dead (11:1–44). Indeed, the writer makes the specific point that Lazarus, who never actually speaks in any of the Gospel accounts, 'was one of those at the table with him' (12:2). The Greek term for 'dinner' here, *deipnon*, is also significant, being used by John on only one other occasion— that of Jesus' last meal with his disciples (translated as 'supper' in 13:2; 21:20). This, along with Jesus' reference to his burial, provides another foreshadowing of the events of his passion to come.

The Gospels have preserved two anointing traditions. The first one is found in Mark 14:3–9, followed closely by Matthew 26:6–13, and carries the association of anointing in preparation for burial. The second tradition, found in Luke 7:36–50, has no associations with burial but focuses rather on the woman's love and respect for Jesus and his forgiveness of her sins. John seems to have combined both traditions in his account: the woman anoints Jesus' feet, as in Luke, but the writer links this action explicitly with Jesus' burial, as do Mark and Matthew.

The location for John's account is identified as Bethany, at the home of Lazarus (12:1); in Mark, Matthew and Luke the incident is situated at the house of Simon (Matthew 26:6; Mark 14:3; Luke 7:40). We know that Lazarus and his sisters were dearly loved friends of Jesus and that he was a regular visitor to their home. This dinner in his honour is clearly a special occasion but menacing clouds accompany the celebration: so many crowds flock to the house to see Jesus and the walking miracle that is Lazarus that the chief priests plan to put both of them to death (John 12:9–10).

When we consider Jesus' earlier visit to Bethany (Monday, Week 2), we encounter an interesting parallel with today's account. During that earlier visit, it was Martha's fretful complaint that Mary was leaving all the work to her that resulted in

Jesus' rebuke. On this occasion there is again a complaint but it comes from Judas Iscariot, not Martha. As before, Martha is busying herself with the practical needs of hospitality and, if she feels any discontent this time, we are not told: maybe she has learned some wisdom from the earlier occasion! Here again, also, Mary has not joined her sister in preparing and serving the meal but is engaged in an activity perceived by at least one of those present as 'useless'. In the earlier incident it was time and Mary's practical energy that were seen as being 'wasted'; here it is the 'costly perfume made of pure nard' which Mary uses to anoint Jesus' feet.

A comparison of the two complaints is of some interest. Martha's complaint in the first narrative, although misplaced, at least had the benefit of being sincere: her desire was essentially to serve Jesus. The same cannot be said of Judas in today's passage. John makes Judas the mouthpiece of an indignant but insincere rant. Why this waste? Wouldn't it have been better to sell the perfume and give the money to the poor? (v. 5). It is obvious from the way the passage has been written that part of the author's intention is to highlight the insincerity and false-hearted character of Judas. While claiming to be concerned about the 'waste' of the perfume that could have been sold to relieve the sufferings of the poor, he sought to obscure his real intention, which was to take what money he could for himself (v. 6).

I do not propose to examine here the writer's possible reasons for portraying Judas in this way, but this picture does serve to throw the single-heartedness of Mary's action of anointing into sharp relief. As on the earlier occasion when she sat at Jesus' feet, oblivious to the complaints of her sister, so here she acts with a complete lack of concern as to what those observing may think of her. Her focus is entirely on

Jesus: she acts spontaneously and instinctively out of her deep love for him, and at that moment it is as if nothing and nobody else exists for her.

John's vivid narrative picture draws us in, gently inviting us to identify with those involved. Alongside Judas, we are asked to own and acknowledge our own tendencies towards insincerity and dishonesty—the times when we benefit or enrich ourselves at the expense of others and the various masks that we so often put on in order to present an over-rosy picture of ourselves to the world. Alongside Mary, we are challenged to examine our priorities and the extent to which we tend to be swayed by other people's opinions. With her, we are encouraged to nurture our loving relationship with Christ and to give our very best to him, and to increasingly look to him as the source of all that is good, joyous and life-giving.

For reflection and prayer

'The eye is the lamp of the body. So, if your eye is healthy, your whole body will be full of light; but if your eye is unhealthy, your whole body will be full of darkness. If then the light in you is darkness, how great is the darkness!'

MATTHEW 6:22–23

Tuesday

Cowardice (1)

Now Peter was sitting outside in the courtyard. A servant-girl came to him and said, 'You also were with Jesus the Galilean.' But he denied it before all of them, saying, 'I do not know what you are talking about.' When he went out to the porch, another servant-girl saw him, and she said to the bystanders, 'This man was with Jesus of Nazareth.' Again he denied it with an oath, 'I do not know the man.' After a little while the bystanders came up and said to Peter,' Certainly you are also one of them, for your accent betrays you.' Then he began to curse, and he swore an oath, 'I do not know the man!' At that moment the cock crowed. Then Peter remembered what Jesus had said: 'Before the cock crows, you will deny me three times.' And he went out and wept bitterly.

MATTHEW 26:69–75

'Pride comes before a fall' goes the old saying, and time and time again the truth of this maxim seems to be expressed in the behaviour and attitudes of Peter. Peter the rash, the impulsive, always so full of enthusiasm and good intentions that he wasn't quite able to carry through. When Jesus walked across the stormy waters of a lake, calling to his terrified disciples in an attempt to reassure them, it was Peter who responded, 'Lord, if it is you, command me to come to you on the water' (Matthew 14:28). With Christ's encouragement he

198

stepped out of the boat and began to walk on the water, but a belated realisation of what he was actually doing frightened him and he started to sink. Earlier (Tuesday Week 4), we saw that Jesus' praise of Peter's acknowledgment of Jesus' divinity at Caesarea Philippi was rapidly followed by rebuke ('Get behind me, Satan!' Matthew 16:23) when Peter revealed that his thinking was all too earthbound. After the last supper it was Peter who at first proudly refused to allow Jesus to wash his feet. Then he capitulated and went overboard ('Lord, not my feet only but also my hands and my head!' John 13:9), leading to Jesus' dryly humorous reassurance that it was only necessary to wash the feet in order to be clean.

So we come to today's sorry episode. In Matthew, the prelude to Peter's threefold denial takes place just before the visit of Jesus and his disciples to the garden of Gethsemane. Jesus' prediction that the disciples will desert him brings forth a characteristic response from Peter: 'Though all become deserters because of you, I will never desert you' (26:33). And when Jesus tells Peter that even he will fail, Peter responds with added vehemence, 'Even though I must die with you, I will not deny you' (vv. 34–35).

Eugene Boring makes an important theological point when he declares Peter to be the representative disciple who serves as both warning and encouragement to us all: 'Even the great Christian leader failed; even the failure repented and became a faithful disciple, entrusted with the Christian mission.'[87] There is truth here, but if we leave it here it is still quite easy for us to hold its challenge at a 'safe' distance. The words of Tom Wright bring things much closer to home:

Denying Jesus is such a sad thing to do. And yet we all do it. Despite the differences of culture and situation, we can even notice parallels, so close as to be almost amusing, between where Peter was that night and where we may find ourselves. A good dinner, plenty of wine… Then a few questions from people we don't even know.

'You're not one of those Jesus-freaks, are you?'

'I mean, nobody here actually believes in Jesus, do they?'

'Well, it's all right to be interested in Jesus, but you don't want to take it to extremes, do you?' [88]

This example has an immediacy and impact that wrench us out of the realm of theory and plunge us directly and uncomfortably into the routine of our daily behaviour and attitudes. I suspect that the example Wright gives can be translated into a whole variety of situations, and that it gives us little room for complacency. Our lives may not be under threat in the way Peter's was, but when we are questioned we may still find ourselves submitting to the more subtle pressures of the need for acceptance and the desire to be liked as we struggle to form our response.

There is a real challenge here concerning the manner in which we outwardly witness to our Christian discipleship, particularly when under pressure. But there is also an inner lesson in humility to be learned, and it is our success or failure in this area that will determine the nature and quality of our external witness (Matthew 7:18). True humility has never been intended as the caricature that is so often pictured or imagined—a sort of self-loathing grovelling in the dust. Rather, humility is a quality that develops naturally and unselfconsciously when we stand in the light and presence of God and are able to see and accept our flawed humanity as it is, rather than as we grandiosely think it should be. True humility confronts us with the reality of both our strengths and weaknesses, our successes and failures, and enables us to contemplate both with equanimity. The extremes of reaction demonstrated so uncomfortably for us by Peter both stem from misplaced pride—an overestimation of his capabilities on the one hand and the tears resulting from wounded pride at his failure on the other.

Paul urged each member of the church at Rome 'not to think of yourself more highly than you ought to think' (Romans 12:3), and his advice holds good for us today. There will be times of success and achievement, but misunderstandings and failures will continue to be a part of our discipleship experience, as they were for Peter (Sunday, Week 5). If we have humility, we will be able to live peaceably with both, within the grace and love of God.

For reflection and prayer

Seek the Lord while he may be found, call upon him while he is near; let the wicked forsake their way, and the unrighteous their thoughts; let them return to the Lord, that he may have mercy on them, and to our God, for he will abundantly pardon.

ISAIAH 55:6–7

Wednesday

Cowardice (2)

While [Pilate] was sitting on the judgment seat, his wife sent word to him, 'Have nothing to do with that innocent man, for today I have suffered a great deal because of a dream about him.' Now the chief priests and the elders persuaded the crowds to ask for Barabbas and to have Jesus killed. The governor again said to them, 'Which of the two do you want me to release for you?' And they said, 'Barabbas.' Pilate said to them, 'Then what should I do with Jesus who is called the Messiah?' All of them said, 'Let him be crucified!' Then he asked, 'Why, what evil has he done?' But they shouted all the more, 'Let him be crucified!'

So when Pilate saw that he could do nothing, but rather that a riot was beginning, he took some water and washed his hands before the crowd, saying, 'I am innocent of this man's blood; see to it yourselves.' Then the people as a whole answered, 'His blood be on us and on our children!'

MATTHEW 27:19–25

Peter and Pontius Pilate don't have a great deal in common but there is one experience that they do share. They are both put on the spot by the unfolding circumstances surrounding Jesus during this Holy Week, and they both find themselves compelled to make a decision between standing up for what they know to be right and taking a cowardly way out in order to protect their own skin. Peter's challenge comes in the unlikely guise of a servant girl in the courtyard of the high priest, who identifies him as one of Jesus' followers; Pilate's comes in the shape of an angry mob, howling for Jesus' blood.

Both men have had some prior warning of the truth of the situation. In response to Peter's over-enthusiasm, Jesus had told him, 'This very night, before the cock crows, you will deny me three times' (Matthew 26:34). Pilate's warning had come through his wife's dream: 'Have nothing to do with that innocent man, for today I have suffered a great deal because of a dream about him' (27:19). For whatever reason, Pilate chooses to ignore his wife's warning—either because the testimony of a woman was not to be taken seriously (compare Luke 24:11) or because the pressure from the crowd is simply too strong.

Pilate does make a half-hearted attempt to persuade the crowd to allow him to release Jesus rather than the criminal Barabbas, but he quickly and easily yields to their demands for Barabbas' release and the crucifixion of Jesus (vv. 21–23). It is at this point that the darkness of Pilate's cowardice takes on a deeper hue and he takes a monumental step further than Peter ever went. 'So when Pilate saw that he could do nothing, but rather that a riot was beginning, he took some water and washed his hands before the crowd, saying, "I am innocent of this man's blood; see to it yourselves"' (v. 24). Here, the experiences of Peter and Pilate clearly diverge: while Peter is ultimately enabled to take responsibility for his actions (see John 21:15–19), Pilate literally 'washes his hands' of the whole business, refusing to take any further responsibility for what is to follow.

This is an ugly episode on every level. We have seen Pilate's cowardice in the face of the crowd; we also see the treacherous manipulation of the crowd by the chief priests and elders as they connive to bring about Jesus' death, and the mindless, primitive bloodlust of the mob. But there is much more in this passage to challenge and disturb us.

When interpreted out of their context, passages such as this have unleashed a torrent of anti-Semitism down the centuries, culminating in the unspeakable horrors of the 20th-century Holocaust. This persecution has taken varying shapes and forms in different historical periods, but in each one the aim has been the same—the condemnation (or, in Hitler's case, the annihilation) of the Jewish people. Whole nations, different sectors within society and the Christian Church itself must accept some share of the responsibility for this. After the horrific experiences of the 20th century, we are able to see some of the issues more clearly, but what we don't always see so clearly is that our human tendency to look for a scapegoat remains. From Adam and Eve onwards, our enthusiasm remains undiminished for shifting the blame in an attempt to show ourselves in a more positive light than we deserve.

So how should we approach this passage and others like it? First and foremost, surely, we should confront the characters within it not as Jews, Romans or whatever but as representatives of the humanity that we all share, with all its strengths and weaknesses. It is when we are unwilling or unable, whether as individuals or as groups, to own the universal fallibility of our human nature that we are in the greatest danger. It is then that we are most likely to make scapegoats of those whom we imagine to be a threat or those whom we simply judge to be 'not like us'.

The scriptures, relentlessly but mercifully, hold a mirror up to our human nature. We are all human and therefore all complicit; we are encouraged to look into that mirror, calmly and without flinching, and then to turn to Christ for our healing, forgiveness and restoration. 'Simon [Peter] son of John, do you love me? ... Feed my sheep' (John 21:17).

For reflection and prayer

[The Lord God said to the man] 'Have you eaten from the tree of which I commanded you not to eat?' The man said, 'The woman whom you gave to be with me, she gave me fruit from the tree, and I ate.' Then the Lord said to the woman, 'What is this that you have done?' The woman said, 'The serpent tricked me, and I ate.'

GENESIS 3:11–13

Maundy Thursday

Treachery

When morning came, all the chief priests and the elders of the people conferred together against Jesus in order to bring about his death. They bound him, led him away, and handed him over to Pilate the governor. When Judas, his betrayer, saw that Jesus was condemned, he repented and brought back the thirty pieces of silver to the chief priests and the elders. He said, 'I have sinned by betraying innocent blood.' But they said, 'What is that to us? See to it yourself.' Throwing down the pieces of silver in the temple, he departed; and he went and hanged himself.

MATTHEW 27:1–5

All the Gospels record the betrayal of Jesus by Judas Iscariot in the garden of Gethsemane (Matthew 26:47–56; Mark 14:43–52; Luke 22:47–53; John 18:1–11), but this short scene is found only in Matthew and it brings the life of Judas to its tragic conclusion. Through virtually all of Christian history, Judas has been held up as an object of horror, of almost universal abhorrence. How *could* he—especially having lived and worked so closely with Jesus for the previous three years—how could he have handed him over to his death in the way that he did?

In our more psychologically conscious age, the questions have become more nuanced, with less inclination to use blanket condemnation as a crude and blunt instrument.

Rather than using such questions to damn Judas, today we are far more interested in asking what might have been going on in Judas' mind as the tragic and desperate events he had largely instigated began to unfold. Our questions are concerned with how to understand, rather than simply rejecting out of hand.

One famous reconstruction of events came from the pen of the English essayist Thomas de Quincey (1785–1859). In his paper of 1852, 'Judas Iscariot', de Quincey sees Judas as no different from his fellow disciples in their general misunderstanding of Jesus' mission: 'Judas Iscariot, it is alleged, participated in the common delusion of the apostles as to that earthly kingdom which, under the sanction and auspices of Christ, they supposed to be waiting and ripening for the Jewish people.'[89]

According to de Quincey's view, where Judas differed from his fellows was not in this area of mistaken belief but in the steps he took in his abortive attempt to make that belief into reality. Judas and the other disciples believed that Israel needed a Messiah who would go on the attack and overthrow their political oppressors. De Quincey's argument is that Judas believed Jesus would fight back if cornered, and so he planned the betrayal simply to force Jesus' hand. When that failed, the enormity of what he had done struck him and he could not live with the consequences.

The cookery writer Delia Smith has another theory. Her feeling is that 'after the kiss, when Judas stood back expecting perhaps chastisement, accusation and anger, what he actually saw in the face of Jesus was an utter lack of condemnation. Instead there was total love and the words "My friend…".'[90] For Judas, the stark contrast between his actions and Jesus' response was too great: such a response could come only from God, and he, Judas, had betrayed him.

Another question that is sometimes raised concerns the differing treatment of Judas and Peter. Judas betrayed Jesus, yes—but we reflected yesterday on how Peter denied him, three times, with increasing vehemence. In today's reading, Judas at least tries to undo the damage his actions have caused; Peter simply went outside 'and wept bitterly' (Matthew 26:75).

Perhaps the chief difference between the two 'betrayals' was one of intention rather than action. Peter often spoke impulsively, blundering around and frequently putting his foot in it, but, as far as we can see, he never attempted to manipulate events or situations to bring about the outcome he felt should result. For all his mistakes and wrong thinking at times, Peter never stopped listening to Jesus. Maybe that's the key to the distinction between the two men, because it seems clear that, somewhere along the line, Judas stopped listening. At some point, his impatience with what he saw as Jesus' hands-off approach boiled over, and his own agenda —which was intended to further what he mistakenly thought would be for the general good—became more important. It could well have been that Judas meant Jesus no harm but simply intended to shock him into taking some kind of decisive action.

Here lies the difficulty, because there are times when we as disciples *are* called by God to act decisively and challenge the status quo. How are we to know whether our impulse is coming from God or from our own unrecognised inner need for love, power or general approval? Such situations often arise in church life. How many of us can put our hands on our hearts and say that we have never attempted to 'tweak' events in order to direct them in the way we thought they should go? From your own experience of church life, just consider for a moment the following diatribe of complaints: 'I don't know how much longer I can stick it at our church. It's too high/too low; it puts too much/not enough emphasis on Holy Communion/the Mass/the Lord's Supper; I don't like the vicar: he/she uses chooses too many/not enough modern choruses in our services—and there's no silence/charismatic worship! Perhaps if I started a contemplative/charismatic prayer group things would be better...'

Does any of this sound familiar? It certainly does to me. Who among us has not, at times, believed that we knew best? Judas may well have believed that he knew best, but his attempt to force the issue had tragic consequences. As disciples, we are called to listen, with deep humility, to God, our own inner stirrings and other people; and these are some of the qualities that Judas appeared to lack. We are indeed fortunate that, by God's grace, our own particular jostlings and jockeyings for position have had a less drastic outcome. 'There but for the grace of God...'

For reflection and prayer

'Let anyone among you who is without sin be the first to throw a stone at her'... When they heard it, they went away, one by one, beginning with the elders; and Jesus was left alone with the woman standing before him.

JOHN 8:7B, 9

Good Friday

When it comes to the crunch...

One of the criminals who were hanged there kept deriding [Jesus] and saying, 'Are you not the Messiah? Save yourself and us!' But the other rebuked him, saying, 'Do you not fear God, since you are under the same sentence of condemnation? And we indeed have been condemned justly, for we are getting what we deserve for our deeds, but this man has done nothing wrong.' Then he said, 'Jesus, remember me when you come into your kingdom.' He replied, 'Truly I tell you, today you will be with me in Paradise.'

LUKE 23:39–43

This tense conversational exchange between Jesus and the men crucified alongside him is recorded only in Luke's Gospel. The fourth Gospel makes reference to two men crucified with Jesus, one on either side (John 19:18). In both Matthew and Mark the references are similar, with the added clarifications that the men were bandits (Mark 15:27; Matthew 27:38) and that both of them taunted Jesus (Mark 15:32; Matthew 27:44). Unlike the case of Barabbas, 'who had been put in prison for an insurrection…and for murder' and whom Pilate had released at the crowd's insistence (Luke 23:18–25), none of the Gospel accounts give any specific information concerning the nature of these men's crimes.

Only in Luke's account is any distinction made between the criminals, or any suggestion that one of them responded to Jesus with penitence and humility rather than taunting and recriminations. Luke is also more specific about the content of the exchanges between Jesus and the two men. The verbal assault of the unrepentant thief is bitter and belligerent: 'Are you not the Messiah? Save yourself and us!' (23:39). His angry attack exposes two interesting points. First, at the point of death, this criminal betrays clearly the general underlying messianic expectation of the time—that the Messiah would come as some kind of conquering saviour whose main concern would be to save both himself and others within the earthly realm.

In some ways, also, the man echoes the taunting challenges of the devil when tempting Jesus in the wilderness: 'If you are the Son of God…' make life easier and more comfortable for yourself! Astonish and amaze the crowds with your miraculous abilities! You won't come to any harm: God will send his angel to save you! But Jesus' teaching always made clear that his kingdom was 'not from this world' (John 18:36). Displays of miraculous pyrotechnics were never part of his agenda, and there was to be no dramatic liberation from the cross, either for Jesus himself or for those who accompanied him.

Secondly, the words and attitude of this angry thief tell us a great deal about his character. It is clear that his encounter with Jesus had taught him nothing. In his mind, the terminal mess he had made for himself was anybody's fault but his own, so it follows that it would also be someone else's responsibility to dig him out. The contrast with the penitent thief could not be more stark. We see in this man, unlike his companion, a total willingness to take personal responsibility for his actions. His life up to this point has clearly gone badly wrong, but here, at the eleventh hour, the awe and love for the God whom he believes will not turn him away triumphantly breaks into his consciousness. 'And we indeed have been condemned justly, for we are getting what we deserve for our deeds' (Luke 23:41a). Here is no beating about the bush, no attempt to squirm out of personal responsibility, no attempt to shift the blame, but simply an honest recognition of Jesus' innocence and undeserved suffering, and a humble plea for his mercy and remembrance. And Jesus' welcome and reassurance are immediate (v. 43).

In the midst of the drama and tragedy of the crucifixion, this telling little incident provides us with an illustration of the Gospel in miniature. Just as Jesus began his ministry by proclaiming good news to the poor and release to the captives (Luke 4:18), so he ends on a note of forgiveness and reconciliation extended to one of those 'poor' who has turned to him. Alan Culpepper comments that, in the Gospel of John, the author stresses the present fulfilment of future hopes concerning life with God.[91] In John, this is demonstrated most clearly when Jesus approaches the tomb of Lazarus and calls him back to life, thus providing a sign of Christ's intention towards all those who turn to him. In Luke, Jesus' words to the penitent thief demonstrate the same intention. But they are meant to be far more than neutrally informative: these, the second set of Jesus' 'words from the cross' in Luke, 'should move every reader to recognise that we, too, stand in need of God's mercy'.[92] As ever, we are not expected simply to remain as observers on the sidelines but rather to become engaged and committed as fully involved participants.

This may be all very well in theory but in practice we are

still left with a disconcerting challenge. Where—if and when it comes to the crunch—do I stand? With the penitent thief or with his craven associate? There is a somewhat clichéd but still uncomfortable question in Christian circles: 'If you were on trial for your life, accused of being a Christian, would there be enough evidence to convict you?' When someone is being commended for some great act of heroism in the face of danger, it is not unusual for the person to play down the courage they have displayed. They may state that they were nothing special, that anyone else in the same situation would have done the same thing. But none of us knows, ahead of such a crisis, how we would react when the chips were really down. We may, at times, succeed in exercising some control over certain aspects of our lives but the time will eventually come when any control we may have had is taken out of our hands. When that time comes and death approaches, whether peacefully or traumatically, the incident in today's reading reminds us that we, too, have a choice to make.

For reflection and prayer

Make me to know your ways, O Lord; teach me your paths...
For your name's sake, O Lord, pardon my guilt, for it is great.
Who are they that fear the Lord? He will teach them the way
that they should choose.

PSALM 25:4, 11–12

Holy Saturday

Staying with the pain

Now there was a good and righteous man named Joseph, who, though a member of the council, had not agreed to their plan and action. He came from the Jewish town of Arimathea, and he was waiting expectantly for the kingdom of God. This man went to Pilate and asked for the body of Jesus. Then he took it down, wrapped it in a linen cloth, and laid it in a rock-hewn tomb where no one had ever been laid. It was the day of Preparation, and the sabbath was beginning. The women who had come with him from Galilee followed, and they saw the tomb and how his body was laid. Then they returned, and prepared spices and ointments. On the sabbath they rested according to the commandment.

LUKE 23:50–56

For some people, the build-up of tension through the tragic drama of Holy Week proves unbearable. Some years ago, a friend of mine told me of her experience of Holy Week in another country. She and her hosts had visited the local church for the Good Friday service, and she was delighted with the experience. The minister had announced at the beginning of the service that he felt they had had enough suffering for one year, so this year they would jump forward and start celebrating Easter right away. So Good Friday in that church resounded to the hearty singing of 'Jesus Christ is risen today—Allelluia!' As one of those who always find

Holy Week very difficult, my friend heartily wished that the church in our own country would follow suit every year.

We may smile and shake our heads or throw up our hands in horror as the inclination takes us, but, either way, my friend's experience confronts us with an important issue. Holy Week, if we take the trouble truly to enter into the sequence of events as they unfold, is always difficult, always painful. It is painful because of what was done to Jesus in our stead; painful also because of what is revealed to us about the weakness and sinfulness of our human nature. But for those who do follow these dramatic events to and beyond the climax of the crucifixion, the same temptation either to 'switch off' or to jump forward presents itself again. Why? Because on this Saturday, we are asked to wait, with no particular hope or expectation. As one of Jesus' followers, not recognising him, said to him on the road to Emmaus, 'But we had hoped that [Jesus] was the one to redeem Israel' (Luke 24:21). This is how it must have felt to those who were with Jesus: there had been such high hopes, but he was dead, and that was all there was to it.

This experience of loss of hope is difficult for us to face, let alone maintain. How different things might feel if events had been so arranged that we were able to celebrate the resurrection immediately after the day of the crucifixion! But no, the tension is maintained and we are asked now to identify with those left behind after Jesus' death—to put ourselves in the shoes of those for whom all hope seemed to have been lost. It's no wonder, perhaps, that we would rather avoid that particular challenge.

It is into this context of waiting without hope that Joseph of Arimathea steps on to the centre of the stage. He is named in all four Gospels and Luke tells us that he was 'a good and righteous man' who, although a member of the council, had not agreed with his colleagues in voting for Jesus death (23:50–51). John's Gospel tells us that Joseph was a disciple of Jesus, though a secret one because of his fear of retaliation (John 19:38), and that he and Nicodemus—another secret disciple—had together taken the body of Jesus and prepared it for burial (vv. 39–40). Mark 15:43 adds the detail that Joseph was highly respected among his fellow religious leaders. It is in Matthew's Gospel that Joseph is declared to be a rich man (27:57) and we are told that the tomb in which he laid Jesus had been intended as his own (vv. 59–60).

As Joseph of Arimathea takes his vital role in the drama, in the midst of an atmosphere of general grief and desolation, Luke's Gospel records something of quiet but deep significance. Joseph, writes Luke, 'was waiting expectantly for the kingdom of God' (23:51)—not 'had been' waiting, but 'was' waiting. Many years before, when Mary and Joseph took the infant Jesus to the temple to present him to God, they were greeted by Simeon and Anna, and there Luke used the same kind of grammatical phrasing when he stated that Simeon was 'looking forward to the consolation of Israel' (2:25). Linguistically it is a tiny point, but amid the darkness it provides a tiny glimmer of light. Joseph of Arimathea had not given up all hope: the expectation was still there and he was still waiting, even as he and Nicodemus prepared Christ's body for burial.

The demands of Holy Saturday ask us to hold ourselves precisely at this point of paradox and tension, neither giving up hope on the one hand nor anticipating what we know is to come on the other. Christ has truly died, and we are invited to hold that realisation in company with those who could have had no idea of the unimaginable miracle that was about to happen. Joseph of Arimathea and his contemporaries lacked what we have but tend to take for granted—the benefit of hindsight. We know, from the biblical witness and the witness of countless numbers of Christians down the ages, that Christ did indeed rise from the dead. Joseph's witness invites us to acknowledge and emulate his decision to continue waiting and believing, despite the apparent hopelessness of the situation. 'Blessed are those who have not seen and yet have come to believe' (John 20:29).

For reflection and prayer

Surely everyone stands as a mere breath. Surely everyone goes about like a shadow. Surely for nothing they are in turmoil; they heap up, and do not know who will gather. And now, O Lord, what do I wait for? My hope is in you.

PSALM 39:5B–7

Easter Day

With fear and great joy

After the sabbath, as the first day of the week was dawning, Mary Magdalene and the other Mary went to see the tomb. And suddenly there was a great earthquake; for an angel of the Lord, descending from heaven, came and rolled back the stone and sat on it. His appearance was like lightning, and his clothing white as snow. For fear of him the guards shook and became like dead men. But the angel said to the women, 'Do not be afraid; I know that you are looking for Jesus who was crucified. He is not here; for he has been raised, as he said. Come, see the place where he lay. Then go quickly and tell his disciples, "He has been raised from the dead, and indeed he is going ahead of you to Galilee; there you will see him." This is my message for you.' So they left the tomb quickly with fear and great joy, and ran to tell his disciples.

MATTHEW 28:1–8

> *'Alleluia! Christ is risen!*
> *'He is risen indeed! Alleluia!* [93]

The triumphant shout of praise that greets the day of Christ's resurrection surely merits the exclamation marks omitted in *Common Worship*. After the hardships of the Lenten journey and the anguish of the events of Holy Week, the intense eruption of light, life and sheer joy is irresistible:

Death's mightiest powers have done their worst,
and Jesus hath his foes dispersed;
Let shouts of praise and joy outburst:
Alleluia!
F. POTT

In the risen Christ, death itself has lost its power and finality, and we are enticed onwards into the divine life in all its richness and mystery. But we need to be on guard at this point, as we may be in danger of doing the entire season, and ourselves, a great disservice. Of course it is right that we celebrate, but if all that happens is that we breathe a metaphorical sigh of relief, thankful that the rigours and discomfort of Lent are over for another year, dive into the chocolate and look forward to getting back to 'business as usual', then we need to ask ourselves what, if anything, has really changed. What has this Lenten journey achieved in me? Am I the same person, spiritually, that I was when I set out on the journey? And if so, what was the point of it all?

Two contemporary theologians offer some helpful and thought-provoking insights into our experience of resurrection joy. In his book *Resurrection*, Rowan Williams reminds us of something we often gloss over in our familiarity with the Gospel accounts—the essential strangeness and unpredictability of the resurrection, through the eyes of those who encountered the risen Christ. In the first instance is the mystery surrounding the resurrection itself: none of the writers can describe it but all are left grappling with the reality of an empty tomb, as today's reading illustrates. Two of the resurrection appearances (to Mary Magdalene at the tomb, in John 20:11–18, and the disciples on the road to Emmaus, Luke 24:13–35) point us to the second mystery—

the unrecognisability of the risen Christ to those who had known him well. These followers were startled into seeing Christ afresh and getting to know him in a radically new way, and, if we will allow him, Christ will continue to confound our own limited expectations too.

> *So the void of the tomb and the unrecognisable face of the risen Lord both speak of the challenge of Easter... The Lordship of Jesus is not constructed from a recollection but experienced in the encounter with one who evades our surface desires and surface needs, and will not subserve the requirements of our private dramas.*[94]

It is right that our joy should be intermingled with a 'holy fear', because the risen Christ who continually invites our allegiance and loyalty refuses to be 'tamed' or made subject to our private whims.

When the Catholic teacher and writer Noel Dermot O'Donoghue writes about the joy of the resurrection, he argues that it cannot be separated from the tribulations that have preceded it: 'In the Apocalypse of John the final joy is described in terms of emergence: "There are they who have come out of great tribulations". The joy is not something that follows on... *it takes its shape from the tribulations; it is inconceivable without the tribulations.*'[95] O'Donoghue goes on to stress that the tribulations are a sharing in the cross of Christ, and remain an integral part of the resurrection that follows. '*The two cannot be separated.* Take away the Cross and you may still have joy but you will not have *this* joy, this kind of joy.'[96] So, to experience the fullness of resurrection joy, the pain and suffering of the cross need not to be thankfully left behind but must somehow be taken up and integrated into the joy of our ongoing journey.

At the beginning of Lent we set out to welcome the way of the cross and to accompany Christ on his road to the crucifixion and beyond. To the level and depth of our involvement the journey will have brought some degree of renunciation, pain, suffering and questioning. There may have been a sharp reality check as we realised afresh that we, in the weakness of our common humanity, are no different from the original disciples. There are times when we fail to keep watch as they failed in the garden of Gethsemane; like them, we also experience times of denial and betrayal, and there are times when we too flee, because we find the challenge to stay with Jesus to the bitter end almost too much to bear. But like them, if we will, we may discover that in the ashes of our failure lie the life-bearing seeds of a hope and future beyond our imagining. The night has indeed passed; a new day has dawned—and the risen Christ beckons us ever onwards.

'Now through the deep waters of death, you have brought your people to new birth by raising your Son to life in triumph. May Christ your light ever dawn in our hearts as we offer you our sacrifice of thanks and praise. Blessed be God, Father, Son and Holy Spirit: Blessed be God for ever.'[97]

For reflection and prayer
While they were talking and discussing, Jesus himself came near and went with them, but their eyes were kept from recognising him.

LUKE 24:15–16

Questions for group discussion

Ash Wednesday to Saturday: Because he first loved us

- 'You are my beloved son/daughter.' At the beginning of our Lenten journey to the cross and beyond, are we able to take these words into our hearts as God's personal affirmation of love for us?
- George Herbert's poem, 'Love (III)', gives us a particularly intense and intimate expression of what 'home' could mean. What kinds of feelings does the poem touch in you? How easy do we find it to allow God to love us in this way?
- 'O Lord, you have searched me and known me... and are acquainted with all my ways.' How do these words of the psalmist make you feel? Do you want God to be 'acquainted with all your ways'?
- In one Gospel account, John is reported as saying of Jesus, 'He must increase, but I must decrease' (John 3:30). How easy do you find it to hand over areas of your work for others to take on?

Week 1: Into the desert

- Spend a little time reviewing the pattern of your life and the subtle shapes and forms that temptation takes within it. How do you recognise temptation when it occurs, and how do you attempt to deal with it?
- How do you hold together the demands of the 'desert' and the demands of the 'marketplace' within your own life? Are there any ways in which the balance could be improved?
- Is there anything in your life that you would identify as 'a thorn in the flesh'? What are you feelings about it, and how do you incorporate those feelings honestly into your prayer?
- Is it possible to live with genuine inner poverty while being materially comfortable? If so, how?
- In order to work towards the healing of divisions in our world, we need to be open to the same work of healing within ourselves. How may we prepare ourselves for such a work of healing?
- Moses encountered God in the burning bush during the course of his normal daily work as a shepherd. Do we expect to encounter God amid the ordinariness of our daily routine?
- Christians across the world and throughout history have been strengthened and inspired by an experience of Christ as Saviour and Friend. How comfortable are you with the 'cosmic Christ' in the prologue of John's Gospel, and how does this image relate to the more intimate picture?

Week 2: Opening the heart in prayer

- In what ways may the Lord's Prayer 'draw us beyond ourselves into the creative and contemplative life of the cosmos'?
- 'The time of business does not with me differ from the time of prayer; and in the noise and clutter of my kitchen… I possess God in as great tranquillity as if I were upon my knees before the Blessed Sacrament.' How might these words of Brother Lawrence help us bring singleness of heart and purpose to all that we do?
- Are you able to identify specific times in your own life when you know you have been fleeing from 'the hound of heaven'?
- How do we stay alongside a person in acute anguish, while at the same time recognising our own helplessness and inability to 'put the situation right'?
- How do you see Jesus' injunction not to judge working out in your own life? Are there situations you can think of that might need some work and prayer in this area?
- What part does imagination play in your spiritual life? Do you expect God to speak to you in and through your hopes, dreams and desires?
- Jesus warned his disciples not to 'heap up empty phrases' (Matthew 6:7) when they prayed. How 'wordy' are our prayers? How comfortable are we in restricting ourselves to a 'prayer word' as the basis for our prayer?

Week 3: Oases of welcome

- Ponder the shape and content of your present life pattern. Is the balance of elements you find there weighted more towards domination or towards stewardship and cooperation?
- Throughout history, trees have been powerful symbols of life, wisdom and continuity. What wisdom can you glean from the trees in your neighbourhood?
- 'Journeying' is a common metaphor for the spiritual life. How deeply does this metaphor speak to your own experience?
- Think of a place that has been of particular significance to you. In what ways has your experience of that place, and your continuing memories of it, nourished your spirit?
- Consider the work/rest balance in your life as it is at the moment. Do any adjustments need to be made?
- Isaiah uses the mountain as a symbol of the unity that will exist between all parts of the creation in God's kingdom. Are there ways in which we can be working towards that unity now?
- Many Christians speak of the strength they receive from being present with Christ in their 'inner cell', even in the midst of activity. Is this a reality in your experience? If not, are there ways in which you could nurture it?

Week 4: Me and my shadow

- What do you think of Jung's concept of the 'shadow'? Does it resonate with any of your own life experience?
- When you are asked to undertake a piece of work, how easy is it simply to focus on the task in hand, without comparing it with what has (or hasn't) been asked of others?
- Who do *you* think that Jesus is? Does the conclusion you come to make any difference to the way you live your life?
- In what ways might our dreams help us to discern the purposes of God in our lives more fruitfully?
- How deeply have you allowed your relationship with God to penetrate your life? Do you have a 'dislocated hip'?
- Do you find the concept of darkness in relation to the spiritual life disturbing or exciting? Why?
- In the Irish tradition, penance was considered not as punishment but as 'medicine for the soul'. How does this approach compare with your own experience?

Week 5: Open to the world

- 'I truly understand that God shows no partiality' (Acts 10:34). To what extent is this true in the life of your own church?
- Philip seems to have travelled around unencumbered. Are we free enough from 'excess baggage' to be able to move where the Spirit may lead?
- Did Christ *really* mean his words in Luke 6? If so, what might they mean for our lives now?
- Have you ever considered seeking spiritual direction? Might this be something that could help and support you on your spiritual journey?
- Can you identify any ways in which the solitary experience is the lot of every human being?
- Thomas Merton wrote, 'The solitary of whom I speak is called not to leave society but to transcend it.' What do you think he meant by this?
- We may assent to the psalmist's declaration, 'You are my God. My times are in your hand.' Do we also agree with it in our hearts, when we consider the reality of our present life experience?

Holy Week

Holy Week has been left free of questions, to allow for deeper personal reflection and meditation on the Bible passage for each day.

Notes

1 A term coined by Melvyn Matthews in his excellent short introduction to contemplative prayer, *God's Space in You* (John Hunt,
   2003), p. 4.

2 R. Alan Culpepper, 'The Gospel of Luke' in *The New Interpreter's
   Bible Vol. IX* (Abingdon Press, 1995), p. 304.

3 Henry Nouwen, *The Return of the Prodigal Son* (DLT, 1992), pp.
   4–5.

4 David L. Bartlett and Barbara Brown Taylor (eds), *Feasting on the
   Word, Year B, Volume 1* (Westminster/John Knox, 2008), p. 249.

5 Eve Baker, *Paths in Solitude* (St Paul's, 1995), p. 20.

6 Ruth Burrows, *Before the Living God* (Sheed and Ward, 1975), p.
   73.

7 Burrows, *Before the Living God*, p. 74.

8 Burrows, *Before the Living God*, p. 74.

9 Burrows, *Before the Living God*, p. 75.

10 Winston Churchill, *Thoughts and Adventures* (Odhams, 1947), p.
   219.

11 Thomas Merton, 'Notes for a Philosophy of Solitude' in *Disputed
   Questions* (Hollis and Carter, 1961), p. 195.

12 Diamuid O'Murchu, *Evolutionary Theology*, cited in Michael
   Leach and Doris Goodnough (eds.), *The Maryknoll Book of
   Inspiration* (Orbis, 2010), p. 100.

13 See D. Sly, *Philo's Perception of Women* (Scholars Press, 1990), pp.
   163–174.

14 From Gregory the Great, *Morals on the Book of Job*, 6, 61.

15 Augustine, Sermon 4, 4.

16 Timothy Fry (ed.), *RB 1980: The Rule of St Benedict* (Liturgical
   Press, 1981).

17 Brother Lawrence, *The Practice of the Presence of God* (Mowbray,
   1980), p. 23.

18 Thomas Keating, *Foundations for Centring Prayer and the Christian
   Contemplative Life* (Continuum, 2007), pp. 296–297.

19 Francis Thompson, 'The Hound of Heaven' www.ewtn.com/library/HUMANITY/HNDHVN.HTM, accessed 7 August 2012.

20 M. Eugene Boring, 'Matthew', in *The New Interpreter's Bible Vol. VIII* (Abingdon Press, 1995), p. 213.

21 Boring, 'Matthew', *NIB Vol. VIII*, p. 211.

22 Fran Herder, *Enter the Story: Biblical Metaphors for Our Lives*, cited in Leach and Goodnough (eds), *Maryknoll Book of Inspiration*, p. 151.

23 John Cassian, *The Conferences* (Newman, 1997), pp. 365–387.

24 Cassian, *Conferences*, p. 383.

25 James Walsh (ed.), *The Cloud of Unknowing*, chapter VII (Paulist Press, 1981), p. 134.

26 Thomas Keating, 'Open Mind, Open Heart' in *Foundations for Centering Prayer and the Christian Contemplative Life* (Continuum, 2007), p. 33.

27 Keating, 'Open Mind, Open Heart', p. 33.

28 Web address www.contemplativeoutreach.org; and for Centering Prayer: www.centeringprayer.com

29 Heinrich Schipperges, *The World of Hildegard of Bingen: Her life, times and visions* (Burns and Oates, 1998), pp. 90–92.

30 Schipperges, *World of Hildegard*, p. 90

31 David Brown, *God and Enchantment of Place: Reclaiming Human Experience* (Oxford University Press, 2004), pp. 85–86.

32 Eva Heymann, *The Deeper Centre* (DLT, 2006), p. 19.

33 See Carolyne Larrington (trans.), *The Poetic Edda* (Oxford University Press, 1996) and Snorri Sturluson, *The Prose Edda* (Everyman, 1987).

34 In S.A.J. Bradley (trans. and ed.), *Anglo-Saxon Poetry* (Everyman, 1992, 1997), pp. 158–163.

35 For information on the Ruthwell Cross, see Éamonn Ó Carragáin, *Ritual and Rood: Liturgical images and the Old English poems of the Dream of the Rood tradition* (The British Library, 2005).

36 Heymann, *The Deeper Centre*, p. 146.

37 Ian Bradley, *Pilgrimage: A spiritual and cultural journey* (Lion, 2009), p. 11.

38 See, for instance, Richard Sharpe, *Adomnán of Iona: Life of St Columba* (Penguin, 1995) and 'The Voyage of Brendan' in Oliver Davies and Thomas O'Loughlin (trans. and eds.), *Celtic Spirituality* (Paulist Press, 1999), pp. 155–190.

39 Sharpe, *Adomnán*, pp. 12–15.

40 Cited in Michelle Brown, *How Christianity Came to Britain and Ireland* (Lion, 2006), p. 115.

41 Susan White, 'The Theology of Sacred Space' in David Brown and Ann Loades (eds), *The Sense of the Sacramental: Movement and measure in art and music, place and time* (SPCK, 1995), p. 31.

42 Janet Backhouse, '"Outward and Visible Signs": the Lindisfarne Gospels' in Brown and Loades (eds), *Sense of the Sacramental*, p. 103.

43 Backhouse, in Brown and Loades (eds), *Sense of the Sacramental*, p. 103.

44 Terence E. Fretheim, 'The Book of Genesis' in *The New Interpreter's Bible Vol. 1* (Abingdon Press, 1994), p. 346.

45 *The Monastery* has since spawned several successors, including *The Convent* (2006) and *The Big Silence* (2010). *The Retreat* (2007) was set in a Buddhist monastery.

46 For further information, see Alastair Lee, *The Forgotten Landscape: Images of Pendle Hill, the Ribble valley and the Burnley area* (Posing Productions, 2003), pp.46–47.

47 *The Journal of George Fox* (Everyman Library, 1924), pp. 59–60.

48 Noel Dermot O'Donoghue, *The Mountain Behind the Mountain: Aspects of the Celtic tradition* (T&T Clark, 1993), p. 30.

49 O'Donoghue, *Mountain Behind the Mountain*, p. 30.

50 Thoreau is best known for his book *Walden* (1854), a reflection upon living a simple life in natural surroundings.

51 Brian Keenan, *An Evil Cradling* (Vintage, 1992), p. 230.

52 Benedicta Ward (trans.), *The Desert Fathers: Sayings of the early Christian monks* (Penguin, 2003), p. 10.

53 From 'September 1968 Circular Letter to Friends', cited in *The Asian Journal of Thomas Merton* (New Directions, 1973), p. xxix.

54 The Beguines (male equivalent, Beghards) were religious lay women who had opted to live lives of chastity and service outside the authority of the recognised religious orders. The movement began in the early 13th century and was chiefly found on the Continent; it continues (though in a greatly altered form) to the present day. Beguines came into being partly as a result of the reluctance of the male religious orders to make any provision for devout women and also from a desire to bring religious life out from behind the walls of the monastery and into the marketplace. See further Saskia Murk-Jansen, *Brides in the Desert: The spirituality of the Beguines* (DLT, 1998).

55 Quoted in Jane Hirshfield (ed.), *Women in Praise of the Sacred* (HarperCollins, 1994), p. 109.

56 For two different academic levels of treatment by the same author, see N.T. Wright, 'The Letter to the Romans' in *The New Interpreter's Bible Vol. X* (Abingdon Press, 2002), pp. 549–590, and Tom Wright, *Paul for Everyone: Romans Part 1: Chapters 1–8* (SPCK, 2004), pp. 126–130.

57 C.J. Jung, *Modern Man in Search of a Soul* (Ark, 1984), p. 137.

58 Boring, 'Matthew', *NIB Vol. VIII*, pp. 344–345.

59 Boring, 'Matthew', *NIB Vol. VIII*, p. 350.

60 Laurens Van de Post, *Jung and the Story of our Time* (Penguin, 1978), p. 9.

61 Terence E. Fretheim, 'The Book of Genesis' in *The New Interpreter's Bible Vol. 1* (Abingdon Press, 1994), p. 568.

62 St Isaac of Syria Skete, Boscobel, Wisconsin, USA.

63 For further information on the Irish *Penitentials*, see Thomas O'Loughlin, *Celtic Theology* (Continuum, 2000), ch. 3, pp. 48–67.

64 'The Penitential of Cummean' in Oliver Davies, *Celtic Theology* (Paulist Press, 1999), p. 230.

65 M. Basil Pennington (ed.), *Aelred of Rievaulx: Treatises and pastoral prayer* (Cistercian Publications, 1971), p. 105.

66 Pennington (ed.), *Aelred*, pp. 110, 111.

67 Minnie Louise Haskin's poem 'God Knows' forms part of a collection entitled *The Desert* and was published in 1908. It

came to popular public attention when King George VI quoted the opening few lines as part of his Christmas broadcast in 1939 ('I said to the man who stood at the gate of the year...').

68 Robert W. Wall, 'The Acts of the Apostles' in *The New Interpreter's Bible Vol. X*, p. 171.

69 Wall, 'Acts of the Apostles' in *NIB Vol. X*, p. 171.

70 In Acts 3, the lame man healed by Peter at the gate of the temple was not a eunuch, but his lameness likewise barred him from the right to enter the temple for worship. The instant he was healed he was free to enter the temple with Peter and John, 'walking and leaping and praising God' (3:8).

71 Susan E. Hylen in David L. Bartlett and Barbara Brown Taylor (eds.), *Feasting on the Word, Year C, Volume 1* (Westminster/John Knox Press, 2009), p. 382.

72 Hylen in Bartlett and Taylor (eds.), *Feasting on the Word, Year C, Volume 1*, p. 384.

73 Daniel Homan and Lonni Collins Pratt, *Radical Hospitality: Benedict's way of love* (Paraclete, 2002), p.158.

74 Burrows, *Before the Living God*, p.74.

75 Homan and Pratt, *Radical Hospitality*, p. 44.

76 Baker, *Paths in Solitude*, p. 96.

77 Baker, *Paths in Solitude*, p. 101.

78 Thomas Merton, 'Notes for a Philosophy of Solitude' in *Disputed Questions* (Hollis & Carter, 1953), pp. 181–182.

79 Baker, *Paths in Solitude*, p. 100.

80 Catherine de Hueck Doherty, *Poustinia* (Fountain, 1997), p. 213.

81 Doherty, *Poustinia*, pp. 21–22.

82 W. Sibley Towner, 'The Book of Ecclesiastes' in *The New Interpreter's Bible Vol. V*, p. 308.

83 C.G. Jung, 'The Stages of Life' (1930) in Joseph Campbell (ed.), *The Portable Jung* (Penguin, 1976), p. 17.

84 Jung, in Campbell (ed.), *Portable Jung*, p. 17.

85 India Hicks in *The Sunday Times* (29 June 2012).

86 Culpepper, 'Gospel of Luke' in *NIB Volume IX*, p. 370.

87 Boring, 'Matthew', *NIB Vol. VIII*, p. 481.

88 Tom Wright, *Matthew for Everyone Part 2: Chapters 16—28* (SPCK, 2002, 2004), pp. 171–72.

89 www.readbookonline.net, accessed 10 August 2012.

90 Delia Smith, *A Feast for Lent* (BRF, 1983), p. 69.

91 Culpepper, 'Gospel of Luke' in *NIB Vol. IX*, p. 459.

92 Culpepper, 'Gospel of Luke' in *NIB Vol. IX*, p. 459.

93 *Common Worship: Services and Prayers for the Church of England* (Church House Publishing, 2000), p. 167.

94 Rowan Williams, *Resurrection* (DLT, 2002), p. 76.

95 Noel Dermot O'Donoghue, *Heaven in Ordinarie: Prayer as transcendence* (T&T Clark, 1979), p. 102, my emphasis.

96 O'Donoghue, *Heaven in Ordinarie*, p. 102, original author's emphasis.

97 *Common Worship*, p. 32.

Also by Barbara Mosse

Encircling the Christian Year

Liturgies and reflections
for the seasons of the Church

The seasons of the Church's year parallel those of the natural world, gifting us with opportunities for spiritual life and growth. The watchfulness of Advent with its symbolism of light and darkness gives way to the explosion of joy as we welcome the birth of Christ; the sombre season of Lent leads us through the despair of the cross to the wonder and joy of Easter; and the weeks of 'Ordinary Time' encourage us to persist in our walk with Christ during those times when nothing much seems to be happening.

Beginning with Advent Sunday, *Encircling the Christian Year* presents a series of short liturgies for each week of the Church calendar, including a Bible reading, reflection and prayers. Special liturgies are also provided for the major festivals and 'red letter days'. The book invites us to deeper prayer, to grow in our relationship with the God who loves us and accompanies us through all the seasons of our lives.

ISBN 978 0 85746 045 5   £9.99
Available from your local Christian bookshop or, in case of difficulty, direct from BRF: please visit www.brfonline.org.uk.

Also from BRF

At the End of the Day

Enjoying life in the departure lounge

David Winter

An octogenarian takes a wryly humorous look at what it's like to be old in an era of the relentlessly new. Turning to the Bible, he explores its store of timeless wisdom, encouragement and reassurance about what it has always meant to grow old and be old. The book is structured around a series of fascinating biblical pictures, from the legendary Methuselah to the feisty Sarah and the great leader Moses, from the picture of inevitable decline as the Preacher saw it in Ecclesiastes to the glorious Nunc Dimittis of old Simeon in the temple.

'At the end of the day' is a well-worn phrase—yet seeing life as a single day, with dawn, noon, sunny afternoon, twilight and then darkness and sleep, provides a sort of contracted chronology of a journey we are all taking. Those who are at, or beyond, tea-time—as well as their friends and family—may find this book offers an essentially optimistic, positive and attractive picture of both the present and the future.

ISBN 978 0 85746 057 8   £6.99
Available from your local Christian bookshop or, in case of difficulty, direct from BRF: please visit www.brfonline.org.uk.

Transformed by the Beloved

A guide to spiritual formation with St John of the Cross

Daniel Muñoz

The 16th-century Spanish mystic John of the Cross is best-known for his reflections on 'the dark night of the soul'. This book explores the dramatic events of his life and times, and also his complex and lyrical poetry, showing how all his work pointed to the reality of God's work through him and presence with him, even in the despair of a prison cell.

Transformed by the Beloved invites us to reflect on different aspects of the Christian journey, all of which John considered crucial for growth in faith and depth of spirituality. John's own experience showed this journey to be at times full of longing and at other times full of the most wonderful shouts of joy. Each chapter ends with suggestions for personal reflection and prayer, with many links to John's poems, new translations of which are included in the book.

ISBN 978 0 85746 584 2   £6.99
Available January 2014 from your local Christian bookshop or, in case of difficulty, direct from BRF: please visit www.brfonline.org.uk.

ENJOYED READING THIS LENT BOOK?

Did you know BRF publishes a new Lent and Advent book each year? All our Lent and Advent books are designed with a daily printed Bible reading, comment and reflection. Some can be used in groups and contain questions which can be used in a study or reading group.

Previous Lent books have included:

When You Pray, Joanna Collicutt
The Way of the Desert, Andrew Watson
Jesus Christ—the Alpha & the Omega, Nigel G. Wright
Giving It Up, Maggi Dawn

> If you would like to be kept in touch with information about our forthcoming Lent or Advent books, please complete the coupon below.

❑ Please keep me in touch by post with forthcoming Lent or Advent books
❑ Please email me with details about forthcoming Lent or Advent books

Email address: _____

Name _____

Address_____

_____

_____

Postcode_____

Telephone_____

Signature _____

Please send this completed form to:

Freepost RRLH-JCYA-SZX
BRF, 15 The Chambers,
Vineyard, Abingdon,
OX14 3FE, United Kingdom

Tel. 01865 319700
Fax. 01865 319701
Email: enquiries@brf.org.uk

www.brf.org.uk

For more information, visit the **brf** website at **www.brf.org.uk**

Enjoyed

this book?

Write a review—we'd love to hear what you think.
Email: reviews@brf.org.uk

Keep up to date—receive details of our new books as they happen.
Sign up for email news and select your interest groups at:
www.brfonline.org.uk/findoutmore/

Follow us on Twitter @brfonline

By post—to receive new title information by post (UK only), complete the form below and post to: BRF Mailing Lists, 15 The Chambers, Vineyard, Abingdon, Oxfordshire, OX14 3FE

Your Details
Name _____
Address_____
_____
Town/City _____ Post Code _____
Email_____

Your Interest Groups (*Please tick as appropriate)	
☐ Advent/Lent	☐ Messy Church
☐ Bible Reading & Study	☐ Pastoral
☐ Children's Books	☐ Prayer & Spirituality
☐ Discipleship	☐ Resources for Children's Church
☐ Leadership	☐ Resources for Schools

Support your local bookshop
Ask about their new title information schemes.